Editor
Jennifer Overend Prior, Ph. D.

Managing Editor
Ina Massler Levin, M. A.

Editor-in-Chief
Sharon Coan, M.S. Ed.

Cover Artist
Brenda DiAntonis

Art Coordinator
Kevin Barnes

Art Director
CJae Froshay

Imaging
Rosa C. See

Product Manager
Phil Garcia

Publishers
Rachelle Cracchiolo, M.S. Ed.
Mary Dupuy Smith, M.S. Ed.

Author

Helen Hoffner, Ed.D.

Teacher Created Materials, Inc.
6421 Industry Way
Westminster, CA 92683
www.teachercreated.com
ISBN-0-7439-3767-8
©2003 Teacher Created Materials, Inc.
Made in U.S.A.

Table of Contents

Table of Contents *(cont.)*

Introduction

Realistic fiction provides a lens through which students can examine their lives and make critical, reflective decisions. The activities, worksheets, book lists, and suggestions contained in *A Look at Realistic Fiction* are appropriate for students in grades 4 to 7 and can be used to enhance instruction with a variety of realistic fiction selections.

A Look at Realistic Fiction is divided into sections to help teachers quickly find appropriate activities and worksheets. The initial sections include:

- Introducing Realistic Fiction
- Historical Fiction
- Narrative Poetry
- The Seuss Connection
- Author Study
- Curriculum Connections
- Closure Activities

These offer lessons and worksheets to guide students before and after they read realistic fiction selections.

The next section, Integrating Technology, offers guidance in using the Internet, DVDs, and videos.

The Unit Management section contains a variety of useful resources, including:

- The Home/School Connection—suggestions for involving parents in their children's literacy progress.

- Reading Log—to assist students in taking notes about the books they have read.

- Thematic Teaching Chart—to assist in planning interdisciplinary lessons by giving titles of realistic fiction, nonfiction, and narrative poems that share common themes.

- Organizing for Instruction—instructional methods and suggestions for lively oral reading activities and vocabulary development.

Students can work independently, in pairs, in small groups, or as a whole class to complete the lessons suggested in this book. Decisions for grouping students are based on many factors. You may find that the students work best independently earlier in the school year. Later in the academic year, when students have learned the classroom routines and expectations, they may be better able to work in pairs or small groups.

Some students prefer to write independently. They enjoy selecting their own topics and controlling the fates of their stories. Other students find motivation by working with peers. They like to express an idea and sharpen their writing with reactions from classmates. While a suggested organization for grouping is given for each lesson in this book, the needs and interests of individual students should guide you in selecting the most productive grouping for each activity.

Today's emphasis on standards-based education has made it essential to list the standards and benchmarks addressed by each lesson. In order to accommodate a wide audience of readers, the McREL Standards (Mid-continent Research for Education and Learning) have been used in this book. You can access the McREL Standards at the Web site: www.mcrel.org/standards-benchmarks

Introducing Realistic Fiction

The first few lessons will enable you to introduce the genre and define the term realistic fiction. Students should come to the awareness that realistic fiction is often based on true events. Because it has a basis in truth, students can relate to the events and characters portrayed in a realistic fiction selection. Students can examine the events portrayed and discuss how these events relate to their own lives.

What If...

See page 6.

In this activity, students learn that they can take an actual event from their lives and create a fictional short story. This helps students examine realistic fiction from the writer's viewpoint rather than the reader's perspective.

Newspaper Fiction: Based on a True Story

See page 7.

This activity expands on the "What If..." activity. In the "What If..." activity, students work with the class to compose a realistic fiction story. In "Newspaper Fiction: Based on a True Story," each student takes an event from a newspaper or magazine and creates a work of realistic fiction based on that true event. This activity requires a student to read and understand a newspaper or magazine article. It also requires the students to go beyond the information presented and to form inferences about the characters and events.

Literary Terms

See page 8.

This activity reviews key terms such as setting, plot, point of view, theme, and main character. Use these terms when conducting lessons using realistic fiction. Students should be able to define and use these terms before proceeding to subsequent activities in this book

What If...

Objective: The student will compose an original story based on a school event.

Standard: Uses the general skills and strategies of the writing process

Benchmark: Writes narrative accounts, such as short stories

Skill Development: Improved sentence structure, use of descriptive vocabulary

Organization: Whole-class activity, pairs, independent work

Materials

- chalkboard
- chalk
- chart paper
- markers

Procedure

1. Begin the unit about realistic fiction by explaining to the students that a realistic fiction story is make-believe, but seems like it could be true. As a group, prepare a story on the chalkboard or on chart paper.

2. Ask the students to dictate sentences about a school event such as a field trip or a school assembly. Then ask questions related to the story, such as:

   - What would have happened if the bus driver had gotten lost as he drove the students on their field trip?
   - What would have happened if the bus broke down on the way to the field trip?
   - What would have happened if the bus broke down on the way back from the field trip?
   - What would have happened if some students had missed the bus coming home from the field trip?
   - What would the students do if a cat or dog jumped on the bus?
   - What would have happened if the teacher forgot to bring the necessary tickets for the field trip?
   - What would have happened if the fire alarm had sounded during the school play?
   - What would have happened if the actors in the school play forgot their lines?
   - What would have happened if the audience walked out during the school play?

3. Compose the story as a group.

4. After writing the group story, invite students to turn true accounts of other school events into examples of realistic fiction. Have the students work individually or in pairs to create stories based on actual events.

Newspaper Fiction: Based on a True Story!

Objective: The student will write a short, fictional story based on a newspaper article.

Standard: Uses the general skills and strategies of the writing process

Benchmark: Uses a variety of prewriting strategies (i.e., makes outlines, uses published pieces as writing models)

Standard: Uses reading skills and strategies to understand and interpret a variety of informational texts

Benchmark: Uses reading skills and strategies to understand a variety of informational texts (i.e., textbooks, news stories)

Skill Development: Writing skills

Organization: Independent activity, pairs, or small groups

Materials

- newspapers (the sports section, in particular)

Procedure

1. Explain that the articles we read in our daily newspapers are true. Sometimes these true stories can give us ideas for creating interesting fiction.

2. Encourage each student to find a brief, intriguing article in the newspaper. (The sports page of a local newspaper often contains stories of high school athletes. Students may find them interesting and easy to understand.)

3. Ask the students if the newspaper articles remind them of any fictional stories they have read recently. Have them discuss the relationship of the news stories to short stories and novels they have read in class.

4. Have students work independently, in pairs, or in small groups to create fictional stories based on actual accounts from the newspaper.

Topic Suggestions for Newspaper Fiction:

The Highs and Lows of the Sporting Life

Look in the sports pages for articles about local high school athletes vying for places on a national championship, world championship, or Olympic team. Follow the progress of the athletes as they compete in qualifying events. Your students can read the news accounts each day and then write realistic fiction stories based on the athletes and the events.

Charitable Acts/Random Acts of Kindness

Newspapers often include stories about young people who serve their communities. The stories of young volunteers can help your students write compelling fiction and may even inspire them to become active in volunteer work. Articles about lost pets, animal rescues, or unusual pet tricks may be appealing to your students and could create interesting situations for realistic fiction.

Young Entrepreneurs

News stories about young people who have launched successful businesses may motivate your students to write short stories and to think about their future careers.

Literary Terms

Objective: The student will identify the setting, plot, point of view, theme, and main characters of the realistic fiction selections they have read.

Standard: Uses reading skills and strategies to understand and interpret a variety of literary texts

Benchmark: Makes inferences and draws conclusions about story elements

Skill Development: Familiarity with the literary terms setting, plot, point of view, theme, and main characters

Organization: Whole-class activity

Materials

- index cards
- markers
- coffee can (decorated)

Procedure

1. It is important for your students to become familiar with literary terms, such as setting, plot, point of view, theme, and main characters.

2. Write each term (setting, plot, point of view, theme, and main characters) on a different index card. Place the cards in a decorated coffee can.

3. Invite a student to select a card from the can.

4. The student reads the card aloud.

5. Then the student thinks of a realistic fiction story and gives a clue, such as, "The setting for the story is Pennsylvania."

6. Other students in the class raise their hands and try to guess the story.

7. When a student gives a correct response, he or she is the next to select a card from the can.

Setting	Plot	Point of View

Theme	Main Characters

Historical Fiction

Historical fiction is one type of realistic fiction. In historical fiction, the author creates characters and then places them against a background of authentic historical events and characters. Historical fiction can help your students identify with children their own age who lived in a particular time period. They will learn the significance of historical events as they explore literary concepts. The activities described in this section reinforce skills in language arts and social studies.

Historical Fiction Book Report
See page 10.

The first page can be used with most works of juvenile historical fiction. Distribute this sheet to help your students reflect on the lifestyle of the main characters in their reading selection. This page will help students think and write about what their lives would have been like if they had lived in the time and place described in the historical fiction selection they read.

What Really Happened?
See page 11.

With this activity students examine a work of historical fiction and determine which events really happened and which events were created by the author. Use "What Really Happened?" (page 12) for this activity.

When You Were Young…
See page 13.

Use this activity in conjunction with a senior citizen day at your school. "When You Were Young…" (page 14) requires each student to interview a senior citizen to learn what life was like when he or she was a child. After interviewing a senior citizen, the students write an historical fiction short story based on the life of the senior citizen. This lesson helps students acquire interviewing skills as well as writing skills.

You Are There!
See page 15.

After reading several examples of historical fiction, the students will write their own historical fiction. Each student will select a familiar time period. The student uses knowledge he or she has gained to write a short story. Allow students to refer to their social studies textbooks to make their short stories historically accurate for details, such as the methods of transportation, ways of cooking, school schedules, and weather conditions in the selected location and time period.

Historical Fiction Book Report

I read the historical fiction selection _____

by _____

This story took place in _____ in the year _____.
(location)

One of the main characters in this selection was a child named _____.

This character's age was _____.

This character's favorite activity was _____

_____.

The character's life was like mine because we both _____

_____

The character's life was different from mine because _____

_____.

Do you wish you lived in that time and place? Why or Why not? Write a paragraph to give your answer.

_____

_____

_____

_____

What Really Happened?

Objective: After reading an historical fiction selection, the student will list facts from the story.

Standard: Uses reading skills and strategies to understand and interpret a variety of literary texts

Benchmark: Makes inferences and draws conclusions about story elements

Standard: Uses the general skills and strategies of the writing process

Benchmark: Writes narrative accounts

Skill Development: Reference skills

Organization: Whole-class activity, independent work

Materials

- student copies of "What Really Happened" (page 12)
- an historical fiction selection, such as *Number the Stars* by Lois Lowry
- reference materials (such as encyclopedia, Internet, social studies textbooks)
- chalkboard
- chalk

Procedure

1. As you discuss a historical fiction selection in your classroom, help your students to determine which events in the story were based on actual historical accounts and which events were created by the author.

2. Read a work of historical fiction with your class. If possible, read a story that relates to a period that your students are studying in social studies classes.

3. Tell your students that when writing historical fiction, authors merge real events with imaginary stories. Some incidents in historical fiction selections have really happened, while other events are imaginary.

4. Ask your students to list the main events of the historical fiction selection. As your students name events, write them on the chalkboard.

5. Next, ask your students which of the events listed on the chalkboard really happened. If the students are not certain, ask them to use social studies textbooks or other reference materials to make the determination.

6. Distribute copies of "What Really Happened?" to your students. Guide them in completing the page.

7. Allow students to share their writings with classmates.

What Really Happened? *(cont.)*

Historical fiction is a type of realistic fiction. In historical fiction, the author creates characters and places them in historical settings.

After reading an historical fiction book, complete the tasks below.

Title: _____

Author: _____

Date of Publication: _____

Setting: The story took place in _____.

(setting and year)

What was the major historical event described in the book?

_____

_____

List three events from the selection that really happened.

_____

_____

_____

List three characters who were real people.

_____

_____

_____

Would you have liked to live in that time period? Why or why not?

_____

_____

_____

How would your life have been different if you had lived in that setting?

_____

_____

_____

_____

When You Were Young...

Objectives: The student will interview a senior citizen.

The student will write an historical fiction story based on an interview.

Standard: Uses listening and speaking strategies for different purposes

Benchmark: Asks questions to seek elaboration and clarification of ideas

Standard: Uses the general skills and strategies of the writing process

Benchmark: Writes biographical sketches

Skill Development: Questioning skills, improved sentence structure, use of descriptive vocabulary

Organization: Small groups or independent activity

Materials

- student copies of "When You Were Young..." (page 14)

Procedure

1. Discuss the importance of senior citizens in the community. Senior citizens provide perspective on changes that have occurred in the community. They can share personal anecdotes about events that students are studying in school.

2. Tell the students that authors often base works of historical fiction on people in their communities and the interesting lives they have led.

3. Explain that their next assignment will be to interview a senior citizen. This might be a grandparent, a neighbor, or a member of the school community. Students can conduct the interviews independently as homework assignments or you might want to plan a trip to an assisted living center to conduct interviews.

4. Distribute copies of "When You Were Young..." to assist students in conducting their interviews.

5. Have the students use the information gathered in their interviews to write factual reports about the people they interviewed. Then have them read aloud and discuss their factual reports with classmates.

6. Instruct each student to use the facts gathered to create a work of historical fiction based on the life of a senior citizen.

7. After the short stories have been completed, you may wish to invite the interviewees to visit the school to share in a writing celebration. (If desired, use this project as part of a school-wide day to honor senior citizens.)

When You Were Young... Worksheet

Interview a senior citizen to learn what schools, jobs, and community activities were like when they were young. Use the questions below.

Schools

1. When you were in my grade level, what year was it?

   _____

2. In what city and state did you live?

   _____

3. Where did you go to school?

   _____

4. How many students were in your class?

   _____

5. What were your favorite books?

   _____

6. Were you involved in sports or clubs at your school? What were they?

   _____

Community Activities

1. What did you and your friends do after school?

   _____

2. What did you do on the weekends?

   _____

3. What kind of music did you like?

   _____

4. Which sports stars or movie stars did you admire?

   _____

Job Opportunities

1. Did you have a part-time job while you were in school?

   _____

2. How much did you earn on your job?

   _____

3. Did you do volunteer work in your community?

   _____

You Are There!

> **Objective:** The student will write an original historical fiction story.
>
> **Standard:** Uses the general skills of the writing process
>
> **Benchmark:** Writes narrative accounts
>
> **Skill Development:** Use of descriptive vocabulary, improved sentence structure
>
> **Organization:** Whole-class activity, independent work

Materials

- historical fiction story
- student copies of "You are There!" (page 16)

Procedure

1. Read an historical fiction story with your class. You might wish to coordinate your study of historical fiction with a unit in your social studies curriculum. For example, when the class is studying the California Gold Rush, your students could read *The Ballad of Lucy Whipple* by Karen Cushman. If your class is exploring the trials and tribulations of frontier families, they might enjoy reading *Sarah, Plain and Tall* by Patricia MacLachlan.

2. After reading an historical fiction story, encourage your students to think about what life was like for children their age in that time period. In *Sarah, Plain and Tall*, two of the main characters, Anna and Caleb, are children. Your students could discuss the chores that Anna and Caleb had to do, their schoolwork, and their participation in social events. Ask your students if they would have enjoyed living in that setting. Why or Why not?

3. Ask your students to imagine what their lives would have been like if they had lived during that time period. How would they get to school? What jobs would they have done around the house?

4. Tell your students that they will each have an opportunity to write a short story about a child living during that time period.

5. Distribute copies of "You Are There!" Worksheet.

6. Guide the students in completing the page. Then encourage the students to use the page as an outline for writing their short stories.

7. Provide time for the students to share their short stories with the class.

You Are There! Worksheet

History is exciting. Many of us wish we could have been present to see events, such as the landing of the first spaceship on the moon or Columbus' voyage to America. Suppose you could travel to another time and place. Where would you like to go? Which historical figures would you like to meet?

If I could travel anywhere in time I would go to:

_____

_____

_____

Event:

_____

_____

Year: _____

Place: _____

I would like to meet an historical character such as _____.

When I met that famous person, I would say, _____

_____

_____

I would help that person by _____.

What do you like to do? Do you like to read and write stories? Do you like to paint? Do you like to play ball? Could you do these things in that place and time?

Create your own historical fiction story where someone your age participates in an historical event.

Use the space below to plan your story. Then write the story on another sheet of paper.

_____

_____

_____

_____

_____

Narrative Poetry

Realistic fiction tells a story. As students read realistic fiction, they become familiar with the story elements of plot, character, setting, point of view, and theme. These elements are also present in narrative poetry. By exploring narrative poetry, students have the opportunity to develop speaking skills as they perform poems for classmates, friends, and family members.

A unit about realistic fiction provides the opportunity for you to introduce the topic of narrative poetry. You can select narrative poems that share the theme of the realistic fiction the students are reading. The chart on pages 71–73 provides a list of themes and related narrative poetry, realistic fiction selections, and nonfiction selections.

The activities in the Narrative Poetry section of this book can provide you with ideas for using narrative poetry in your classroom.

Tell Me a Story, Read Me a Poem
See page 19.

This is an introductory activity which explains the concept of narrative poetry. Students demonstrate their understanding by completing a worksheet that asks them to identify the theme, setting, main characters, point of view, and plot of a narrative poem.

Tell Me a Story, Write Me a Poem
See page 20.

This activity shows students that they can write narrative poems based on events in their own lives.

The Prose and Poetry Connection
See page 21.

This lesson helps students draw parallels between the realistic fiction they are reading and narrative poetry. In this activity, each student is asked to write a narrative poem based on a realistic fiction story. This activity gives students an opportunity to reflect upon their reading and offer creative responses.

Poems and Prose on Stage
See page 22.

This lesson encourages students to develop their oral reading abilities. This activity encourages students to read selections of narrative poetry and related realistic fiction for their classmates. This develops speaking and listening skills for all members of the class.

Narrative Poetry *(cont.)*

Objective: The student will identify story elements (plot, character, setting, point of view, and theme) in a narrative poem.

Standard: Uses the general skills and strategies of the reading process

Benchmark: Understands the use of language in literacy works to convey mood, images, and meaning

Skill Development: Identifies plot, characters, setting, point of view, and theme

Organization: Whole-class activity, independent work

Materials

- copies of narrative poems for each student
- student copies of "Tell Me a Story, Read Me a Poem!" (page 19)

Procedure

1. A unit about realistic fiction provides an opportunity for you to introduce the topic of narrative poetry. You can select narrative poems that share the theme of the realistic fiction the students are reading.

2. Begin by telling your students about a funny or unusual incident that happened to you.

3. Ask your students if they would like to share a story with the class. Provide time for students to come to the front of the room to share stories.

4. Introduce the term *narrative poetry*. Tell the class that a narrative poem is a poem that tells a story.

5. Read a narrative poem to the class. You may wish to begin with a well-known dramatic poem, such as "Paul Revere's Ride" by Henry Wadsworth Longfellow or a humorous poem, such as "The Walrus and the Carpenter" by Lewis Carroll. The chart on pages 71–73 can guide you in selecting narrative poems to correspond with the realistic fiction subject your class is reading. Be sure to provide students with copies of the poems, so that they can follow the text as you read.

6. Help the student identify the story elements (plot, character, setting, point of view, and theme) contained in the narrative poem.

7. Distribute copies of "Tell Me a Story, Read Me a Poem!" Ask the students to complete the "Tell Me a Story, Read Me a Poem!" page. Students can complete the page independently or work in groups of three to four.

Tell Me a Story, Read Me a Poem!

A narrative poem is a poem that tells a story. Perhaps you know famous narrative poems, such as, "A Visit from St. Nicholas" (or "'Twas the Night Before Christmas"), "Casey at the Bat", or "Paul Revere's Ride."

Read the narrative poem given to you in class. After reading the poem, complete the page.

Poem Title: _____

Poet: _____

Theme: _____

Setting: _____

Main Characters: _____

_____

Point of View: _____

(First, Second, or Third Person)

First person—the poet uses the word I and acts as the storyteller.

Second person—the poet uses the word you.

Third person—the poet uses pronouns such as he or she.

Plot (What happened?) :

_____

_____

_____

_____

_____

_____

_____

_____

_____

_____

_____

_____

Tell Me a Story, Write Me a Poem!

Objective: The student will write a narrative poem.

Standard: Uses the general skills and strategies of the writing process

Benchmark: Writes narrative accounts

Skill Development: Improved sentence structure

Organization: Pairs, independent work

Materials

- copies of narrative poems

Procedure

1. Read several examples of narrative poems with the class. Discuss the poets' style and use of descriptive language.

2. Remind the students that narrative poetry tells a story and that everyone has stories to tell.

3. Ask the students to work with a partner. Have each student turn to a partner and tell a story.

4. Now ask the students to return to their own seats. Tell the students that they will have an opportunity to transform their stories into narrative poetry.

5. Tell the students that a narrative poem usually has several stanzas. A stanza has one main idea. Tell each student to think about the story he or she will transform into a narrative poem. The student should think about the main events of their story and plan one event for each stanza. (Note: The students have been studying realistic fiction. Tell the students that the narrative poems they write do not have to be true stories. They might want to embellish their true story and make their narrative poems works of realistic fiction.)

6. Instruct the students to write the main events of their stories and then use those lists as outlines for their narrative poems.

7. Provide time for the students to write their narrative poems. Circulate the classroom to assist students and offer guidance.

8. Invite the students to read their completed narrative poems for their classmates.

Prose and Poetry Connection

Objective: The student will write a narrative poem based on a prose realistic fiction selection.

Standard: Uses the general skills and strategies of the reading process

Benchmark: Reflects on what has been learned after reading and formulates ideas, opinions, and personal responses to texts

Standard: Uses the general skills and strategies of the writing process

Benchmark: Writes narrative accounts

Skill Development: Improved sentence structure

Organization: Whole-class activity, independent work

Materials

- narrative poems
- paper
- chalkboard
- chalk

Procedure

1. Select a narrative poem that has a similar theme to the realistic fiction topic your class is reading. For example, you might select the narrative poem, "Casey at the Bat" when your students are reading *Catcher with a Glass Arm* by Matt Christopher or you could read "Paul Revere's Ride" when your students are reading *Johnny Tremain* by Esther Forbes.

2. Tell the class that you would like to help them construct narrative poems based on the realistic fiction they are reading.

3. Ask the students to name the main idea of the realistic fiction selection the class has been reading. Then tell the students that you are going to list main events from the selection in sequence.

4. Ask the class what happened first in the story, what happened next, etc. List the events in phrases rather than with complete sentences.

5. There will now be an outline on the chalkboard for the students to follow. Tell the students that they are ready to begin a first draft of their poems.

6. Encourage the students to use one event on the chalkboard for each stanza.

7. Provide time for the students to share their poems with classmates.

Poems and Prose on Stage

Objective: The student will read selections of prose realistic fiction and narrative poetry expressively for their classmates.

Standard: Uses reading skills and strategies to understand and interpret a variety of literary texts

Benchmark: Makes oral presentations to the class

Skill Development: Oral expression

Organization: Whole-class activity, small groups

Materials

- realistic fiction stories
- narrative poems
- costumes and props
- video camera or cassette recorder

Procedure

1. Give your students the opportunity to read narrative poems and realistic fiction stories.

2. Pair a work of realistic fiction with a narrative poem that has the same theme. For example, you might use the narrative poem, "Casey at the Bat" by E.L. Thayer and *The Lucky Baseball Bat* by Matt Christopher.

3. Discuss the differences between prose and poetry. *Prose* refers to written or spoken language that resembles everyday speech. Prose is often defined as writing that is not verse. The realistic fiction novels suggested throughout this book are examples of prose. The term *poetry* refers to spoken or written language that has a specific meter. Poetry may have a rhyming pattern as in "Take a look, Here's a great book." Poetry may also be free verse. Free verse is poetry that does not rhyme.

4. Divide students into groups of four. Give some groups a narrative poem and give other groups a prose realistic fiction selection. Ask each group to select a stanza or paragraph that they would like to read expressively for their classmates.

5. Provide time for the group members to select and practice the text that they would like to read. Provide costumes and props, if appropriate.

6. Videotape the oral readings so students can critique and improve their speaking ability. If a video camera is not available, you may wish to make an audio tape of the performance.

The Seuss Connection

Ted Geisel, better known as Dr. Seuss, was known for writing and illustrating books, such as *Green Eggs and Ham* and *The Cat in the Hat*, for beginning readers. Dr. Seuss, however, wrote many books with messages for older children and adults. *You're Only Old Once* is recommended for children over age 70. *Oh, the Places You'll Go* has become a popular high school and college graduation gift.

Dr. Seuss wrote narrative poetry. He told stories in rhyming verse. The book titles listed below contain appropriate messages for older students. The activities that follow encourage students to examine Dr. Seuss' narrative poetry and make connections to the realistic fiction selections they are reading.

Recommended Dr. Seuss Titles for Older Students	
Title	Topic
The Lorax	Protecting the Environment
How the Grinch Stole Christmas	Commercialism during the holidays
The Butter Battle Book	War
The Sneetches and Other Stories	Prejudice and racial stereotyping
Horton Hears a Who	Protecting the rights of those less fortunate
Horton Hatches the Egg	Faithfulness
Oh the Places You'll Go	Setting High Goals

The Dr. Seuss Connection

Objective: The student will give an oral report of a book written by Dr. Seuss.

Standard: Uses reading skills and strategies to understand and interpret a variety of literary texts

Benchmarks: Understands the use of language in literary works to convey mood, images, and meaning

Standard: Understands inferred and recurring themes in literary works (i.e. bravery, loyalty, friendship, good vs. evil; historical, cultural, and social themes)

Benchmark: Makes connections between the motives of characters or the causes for complex events in texts and those in his or her own life

Skill Development: Summarizing, identifying the main idea, speaking skills

Organization: Whole-class activity, small groups

Materials

- several Dr. Seuss books (including *The Lorax, The Sneetches and Other Stories,* and *The Butter Battle Book*)
- copies of Oh, The Lessons You'll Learn (Activity Guide), pages 25 and 26

Procedure

1. Read Across America Day is celebrated every year on or near Dr. Seuss' birthday, on March 2. This day is a day to celebrate and encourage reading.

2. Schedule a Dr. Seuss day in your classroom. Invite the students to bring their favorite Dr. Seuss books. Begin by asking each student to name his or her favorite Dr. Seuss book.

3. Ask the students, "Why did you enjoy Dr. Seuss books when you were a young child?" "What makes Dr. Seuss books special?" The students might say that they enjoyed the rhyming nature of Dr. Seuss' books.

4. Tell the students that Dr. Seuss often wrote narrative poetry. He told stories using rhyming verse. Review the concept of narrative poetry.

5. Display copies of *The Lorax, The Sneetches and Other Stories,* and *The Butter Battle Book.* Tell the students that Dr. Seuss wrote these books as narrative poetry. These books deal with topics that older students can understand and discuss.

6. Tell the students that they will be working in groups to read and discuss books written by Dr. Seuss.

7. Divide students into groups of three to six. Give each group time to select a Dr. Seuss title to read and discuss.

8. Distribute copies of "Oh, The Lessons You'll Learn." Ask each group to complete page 26.

9. Ask each group to make an oral report to the entire class. In the oral report, each group should:

    —Give a summary of the book read.

    —Identify and discuss the lesson contained in the book.

Oh, The Lessons You'll Learn

Dr. Seuss? Yes, you probably read Dr. Seuss books when you were very young. Did you know that Dr. Seuss also wrote books for older students and adults? One of his most popular books, *You're Only Old Once*, is recommended for people over age 70! Many Dr. Seuss books contain messages for older students.

Directions:

1. Work with a group of your classmates. Select one of the Dr. Seuss titles listed below.

   The Lorax

   The Sneetches and Other Stories

   Horton Hears a Who

   Horton Hatches the Egg

   The Butter Battle Book

   How the Grinch Stole Christmas

   Oh, The Places You'll Go

2. Read the book. Discuss the book with members of your group. Consider these questions as you discuss the book:

   - Who were the main characters in the book?
   - Did these characters appear in any other books by Dr. Seuss?
   - Could you classify the actions of these characters as good or evil?
   - Do you have a friend who would enjoy this book?
   - Why would this book be appropriate for your friend?
   - Why do you think Dr. Seuss wrote this book?
   - What was the main idea of the book?
   - What lesson was revealed in this book?
   - When was this written?
   - Is the lesson appropriate for today's students?

3. Complete the page given to you in class.

4. Prepare an oral report to present to the entire class. Summarize the book for the class and state the lesson in that book.

   - State the main idea of the book.
   - State the events that occurred in the book.
   - Describe the main characters.
   - What did they look like? What were their special qualities? What did they do that made them memorable?
   - State the lesson presented in the book.
   - What can we learn by reading this book?

Oh, The Lessons You'll Learn Summary

Group Members: _____

Dr. Seuss story: _____

Copyright date: _____

Summary of the Book: _____

_____

_____

_____

_____

_____

Topic of the Book: _____

Lesson of the book: _____

_____

_____

_____

_____

_____

_____

26

Finding Related Literature

Objective: After hearing a narrative poem, the student will list prose realistic fiction with similar themes.

Standard: Uses reading skills and strategies to understand and interpret a variety of literary texts

Benchmarks: Makes inferences and draws conclusions about story elements

Uses reading skills and strategies to understand a variety of literary passages and texts

Skill Development: Forming inferences, recognizing related themes

Organization: Whole-class activity, small groups

Materials

- several books by Dr. Seuss (see chart on page 28)
- realistic fiction books (see chart on page 28)

Procedure

1. The writing of Dr. Seuss is fanciful and takes place in an imaginary world. Dr. Seuss, however, explored topics such as racial prejudice and ecology that directly affect the lives of older students.

2. Encourage the students to make a connection between a Dr. Seuss book and a work of realistic fiction. See the chart below for themes, Dr. Seuss titles, and related realistic fiction books.

3. Select a theme from the chart.

4. Read the corresponding Dr. Seuss narrative poetry selection aloud to the class.

5. Discuss the poem with the class. Ask the students, "What was the message of that poem?"

6. Ask the students if they have read any novels with similar messages. Assist them in making lists of related realistic fiction titles. (You may want to allow them to ask the librarian, other teachers or students for suggested books.)

7. Guide the students as they read realistic fiction selections related to the theme.

Finding Related Literature *(cont.)*

Theme	Dr. Seuss Title	Related Realistic Fiction
Racial Prejudice	The Sneetches and Other Stories	Number the Stars Roll of Thunder, Hear My Cry
Ecology	The Lorax	The Talking Earth
Setting High Goals	Oh, The Places You'll Go	Stone Fox The Secret School Where the Red Fern Grows
Protecting the Rights of Those Less Fortunate	Horton Hears a Who	Maniac Magee
Commercialism at the Holidays	How the Grinch Stole Christmas	The Best Christmas Pageant Ever
Friendship and Faithfulness	Horton Hatches the Egg	Bridge to Terabithia
War	The Butter Battle Book	Amelia's War
Positive Thinking	Did I Ever Tell You How Lucky You Are?	Loser
Hospitality/Finding a Home	Thidwick, the Big Hearted Moose	Gold in the Hills
Indecision	Hunches in Bunches	Addie's Long Summer
Perserverance	McElligot's Pool	Pictures of Hollis Woods
Greed	Yertle the Turtle and Other Stories	Hoops
Contentment	I Had Trouble in Getting to Solla Sollew	The Cat Ate My Gymsuit

Read Aloud

Objective: The student will read prose and narrative poetry expressively for their classmates.

Standard: Uses the general skills and strategies of the reading process

Benchmark: Establishes and adjusts purposes for reading

Skill Development: Oral expression, fluency

Organization: Whole-class activity, small groups

Materials

- several books by Dr. Seuss
- realistic fiction stories
- cassette recorder

Procedure

The lyrical narrative poetry of Dr. Seuss provides a wonderful read-aloud adventure. Realistic fiction can be read dramatically and can provide a spine-tingling, heart wrenching moment. Encourage your students to work in groups to create a memorable day of oral reading.

1. Ask the students to work in groups of four. Give each group one Dr. Seuss book and one realistic fiction story that share a common theme.

2. Ask the groups to select a segment from the realistic fiction story that they would like to read aloud to their classmates. Encourage them to select a segment that provides a great deal of emotion and reveals the nature of the characters.

3. Have the students prepare to read the segments aloud. The Dr. Seuss segments can be read in their entirety. Students should select one to two pages from the realistic fiction story to read.

4. Have two students in the group practice reading the Dr. Seuss story while two other students in the group practice reading the chosen segment from the realistic fiction story.

5. Ask the groups to read their selections aloud for the entire class. Tape record performances on an audio tape and make them available for listening in the classroom library.

Author Study

Meet the people behind the words. Conduct author studies to help your students learn about the lives of their favorite authors. When they learn about an author's interests, education, and writing habits, the students are able to identify with that author. The students will see the authors as people like themselves who enjoy telling stories. This may encourage them to view themselves as writers and build confidence in their writing ability. The activities in this section will help you conduct author studies with your class.

I'd Like to Introduce…
See page 31.

This lesson presents the topic of author studies and invites students to learn more about their favorite authors.

Letter to My Favorite Author
See page 32.

This activity will help students develop skills in letter writing and encourages students to form questions that they would like to pose to their favorite authors.

Dedication Detective
See page 34.

This is an activity that suggests that students can sometimes learn a great deal about an author by examining the dedications found in their books.

Author Survey
See page 37.

The Author Survey activity encourages students to survey their classmates to determine the most popular books of a given author.

Library Survey
See page 40.

The library survey activity takes the students' research to a larger scale. To complete the survey, students must interview the school librarian to determine the reading interests of members of the entire school rather than just their classmates.

I'd Like to Introduce...

Objective: The student will create questions to ask their favorite authors.

Standard: Uses listening and speaking strategies for different purposes

Benchmark: Asks questions to seek elaboration and clarification of ideas

Standard: Gathers and uses information for research purposes

Benchmark: Uses a variety of resource materials to gather information for research topics

Skill Development: Improved sentence structure, research techniques

Organization: Whole-class activity

Materials

- computer with Internet access
- chart paper
- markers

Procedure

1. Select an author to present to your class. You might select an author based on the popularity of his or her books with your students or you may wish to present an author who lives in your area.

2. Bring several of the author's books to class. Tell the students that you would like to help them learn more about the author before reading the books.

3. You can gather information about the author by reading the brief biography of the author on a book jacket. You can also enter the author's name in an Internet search engine to locate information. Biographical information on the authors can often be found on a publisher's Web site. Library reference books contain information on children's authors as well.

4. Share information about the author with your students. You may wish to tell students the author's age, interests, writing habits, and other facts that you gathered from your research.

5. Ask your students to think of questions they may have about the author. Write the questions on chart paper and display the chart in the classroom. Tell the students that they may find the answers to these questions as they complete the remainder of the activities in the author study unit.

Letter to My Favorite Author

Objective: After reading a realistic fiction story, the student will write a letter to the author.

Standard: Uses the general skills and strategies of the writing process

Benchmark: Writes business letters and letters of request and response (i.e. uses business-letter format; states purpose of the letter; relates opinions, problems, requests, or compliments; uses precise vocabulary)

Skill Development: Writing a letter

Organization: Whole-class activity, independent work

Materials

- computer with Internet Access
- paper and pens for writing letters
- envelopes
- stamps
- student copies of "Letter to My Favorite Author" (page 33)

Procedure

1. After reading a novel, encourage your students to write letters to the author. While e-mail may be a quick means of communication, students also need practice in writing formal letters. By writing a letter to an author, students will take time to compose their thoughts and master the form of writing a letter.

2. There are many ways to find an author's address. You can enter an author's name on an Internet search engine. This should lead to a publisher's page listing an address to send mail to the author. You can also find publisher addresses in the book. Publishers can forward the letters to the author.

3. Guide your students as they complete the "Letter to My Favorite Author" page and write their letters.

4. Students need to feel that their work has meaning. Be sure to mail the letters your students write. The letters should not be viewed as simply a homework assignment or classroom exercise to be added to the student's portfolio. (If you do wish to add the letters to the student's portfolio, make a copy and send the original letter to the author.) Be sure to have students use your school address as a return address in order to protect their privacy.

Letter to My Favorite Author *(cont.)*

All of us enjoy receiving comments about our writing. Authors want to know what you think about their books, too. Did you like the ending? Would you have written a different ending? Would you like the author to write a sequel?

1. Write a letter to the author of a realistic fiction story that you enjoyed.

2. In your letter, tell the author why you liked this book. Tell the author if you would like to read a sequel to this book.

3. You may wish to ask the author some of the following questions:
   - How did you get the idea for this book?
   - Did you model the main character after someone you know?
   - How long did it take you to write this book?
   - Do you write at home or in an office building?
   - How much time do you spend writing each day?
   - Do you like to write in the morning, afternoon, or evening?
   - Do you write with pen and paper or do you use a computer to write your stories?

4. Use the format shown below to write your letter.

Street Address
City, State, Zip Code

Date

_____,
Salutation

Body of the Letter

Closing,
Signature

Dedication Detective

Objective: The student will read the dedication of a realistic fiction story and discuss the ways in which the dedication relates to the author's life.

Standard: Uses the general skills and strategies of the reading process

Benchmark: Reflects on what has been learned after reading and formulates ideas, opinions, and personal responses to texts

Skill Development: Research skills, forming inferences

Organization: Whole-class activity, pairs, small groups, or independent work

Materials

- realistic fiction stories
- student copies of "Dedication Detective" (page 36)

Procedure

1. When introducing a novel to your class, preview the book by having the students glance through it. Ask students to look for an introduction and for information about the author's life that would contribute to students' understanding and enjoyment of the novel.

2. At the conclusion of the preview, help students locate the dedication in the book. (This is usually contained in the first few pages.)

3. Explain that book dedications provide a window into an author's private life. In their dedications, authors often thank their spouses, parents, children, and editors for offering support throughout the writing process. Sometimes authors repeat a line from the book or make reference to a character's habits. Example:

   > *Jerry Spinelli dedicated his 1996 novel, Crash, "To Carl Francis, who has danced on the scoreboard." Crash tells the story of a football hero whose accomplishments light up the neighborhood scoreboard. The dedication of this novel relates to the main idea of the novel. Invite your students to read the dedications of several books.*

4. After reading the dedication, guide students in forming inferences. How does the dedication relate to the message of this book? Could there be parallels between the characters in the novel and the people to whom this book is dedicated? To whom is the author dedicating this book? Why?

Dedication Detective *(cont.)*

5. Share the following with the students.

   *Gail Rock dedicated her novels, The House Without a Christmas Tree and The
   Thanksgiving Treasure to "Grandma and Dad." Rock's books tell the story of
   Addie, a motherless young girl living with her grandmother and her father.
   The grandmother, father, and Addie are the main characters in these novels.
   The dedication suggests that the author is thanking members of her own family
   for the love and guidance that led to her becoming a writer. This book may be
   semi-autobiographical.*

6. After reading a novel with your students, return to the dedication. The students will then be ready
   to answer the questions raised in step 4.

7. Instruct students to complete "Dedication Detective."

Dedication Detective Worksheet

Book Title:_____

Copy the dedication of this story below.

_____

_____

_____

_____

_____

To whom does the author dedicate this novel? _____

Does the author tell the reader how this person is related to him or her? _____

Is the book dedicated to the author's parents, a child, a spouse, or to the editor?

_____

_____

The people mentioned in the dedication could be like the characters in the book. What character in the book could be like the person for whom this book is dedicated?

_____

In what ways could the person in the dedication and the character in the book be similar?

_____

_____

_____

_____

_____

Author Survey

> **Objective:** The student will gather data and construct a graph.
>
> **Standard:** Gathers and uses information for research purposes
>
> **Benchmark:** Gathers data for research topics from interviews
>
> Organizes information and ideas from multiple sources in systematic ways (i.e., time lines, outlines, notes, graphic representations)
>
> **Skill Development:** Conduct interview, construct graphs
>
> **Organization:** Whole-class activity, small groups

Materials

- copies of "Author Survey" (page 38)
- copies of "Author Survey Graph" (page 39)

Procedure

1. As you discuss reading selections with your students, you will begin to notice which authors have become their favorites. Compile a list of your students' favorite authors.

2. Define the word *survey* for your students. Ask them if anyone has ever approached them at a shopping mall or another public place to ask their opinions for a survey. Discuss telephone surveys, mall surveys, and other ways researchers gather information.

3. Tell your students that they will each have the opportunity to conduct a survey with their classmates.

4. Divide the students into groups of three to five. Give each group the name of an author (from the list compiled in step 1).

5. Distribute "Author Survey" and "Author Survey Graph."

6. Ask each group to read the directions.

7. Each group must write the titles of the books written by the assigned author on the author survey chart. The students may need to visit the school library to find the titles written by each author.

8. Provide time for the students to survey their classmates.

9. When the surveys have been completed, help the students calculate the responses.

10. Help the students make graphs to show their data using the Author Survey Graph.

Author Survey Form

1. Write the name of an author on the line below.
2. Write the names of up to 4 books by the author.
3. Record each students' name on the chart.
4. Write an x to indicate each student's favorite book by the author.

Author _____

Student Names	Book Title 1	Book Title 2	Book Title 3	Book Title 4

38

Author Survey Graph

1. Use the information gathered on page 38 to make a graph below.
2. Write the author's name and book titles below.
3. Below each title color a space for each student's favorite book.

_____ Author

	Title:	Title:	Title:	Title:
11				
10				
9				
8				
7				
6				
5				
4				
3				
2				
1				

Library Survey

> **Objective:** The student will gather data and construct a graph.
>
> **Standard:** Uses listening and speaking strategies for different purposes
>
> **Benchmark:** Asks questions to seek elaboration and clarification of ideas
>
> **Standard:** Gathers and uses information for research purposes
>
> **Benchmark:** Gathers data for research topics from interviews
>
> Organizes information and ideas from multiple sources in systematic ways (i.e., timelines, outlines, notes, graphic representations)
>
> **Skill Development:** Conduct interviews, construct graphs
>
> **Organization:** Whole-class activity, small groups

Materials

- student copies of "Library Survey" (page 41)

Procedure

1. Meet with your school librarian to discuss the realistic fiction that your students are reading. Invite the librarian to visit the class to share other works by the students' favorite authors.

2. After the librarian's visit, tell the students that you would like to help them determine which are the most popular books in the school. To do this, the students will have the opportunity to interview the librarian to get his or her opinion about the most popular books.

3. In preparation for the interview, help your students make a list of appropriate questions for the librarian.

4. Divide the students into groups of three to five. Have each group select an author from the list contained on the "Library Survey" page.

5. Provide time for the students to interview the school librarian. Students should meet with the librarian in their groups. Group members should take the "Library Survey" page with them for the interview.

6. Instruct the students to confirm this information by examining records of school library use.

Library Survey *(cont.)*

What are the most popular books in the library? Authors, such as Jerry Spinelli, Richard Peck, and Judy Blume have written many books. If you ask the authors, they will usually tell you which of their books are their own favorites.

Conduct a survey to learn which books are the most popular in your school. Follow the directions below to conduct your survey.

1. Select an author from the list below.

   - Richard Peck
   - Paula Danziger
   - Beverly Cleary
   - Lois Lowry
   - Katherine Paterson
   - Rosemary Wells

   - Jerry Spinelli
   - Judy Blume
   - Patricia MacLachlan
   - Matt Christopher
   - Louis Sachar
   - Ann Martin

2. Ask the school librarian if your group could meet with him or her to ask questions about the books students select in the library.

3. Go to the school library. Use the card catalog or library computer database to make a list of all the books by that author in the school library.

4. Tell the librarian that your group is conducting a survey and tell the librarian the name of the author your group has selected. Ask him or her if there is a way to determine how often that author's books are checked out of the library. Ask the librarian if he or she could show you the number of times each book has been checked out.

5. Make a graph showing the number of times each book has been checked out from the library.

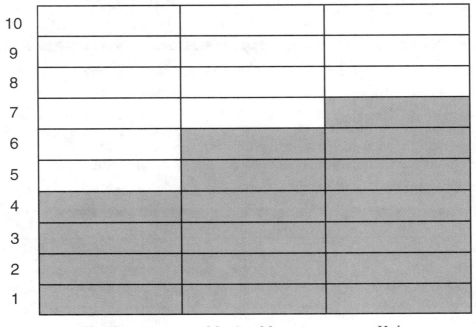

Curriculum Connections

The activities in this section can help you to integrate realistic fiction stories into your science, social studies, and math instruction. Effective teachers pair fiction and nonfiction titles to give students background about topics and to link topics across curricular areas.

Theme Song Time
See page 43.

With this activity, students match the themes of songs to pieces of realistic fiction.

Is That True?
See page 44.

Students will put their research skills to use with this activity. They will use reference materials to determine which people, places, and events in realistic fiction are true and which ones are imaginary.

Map it Out
See page 46.

While reading realistic fiction stories, the students will have the opportunity to track the locations in the story on maps.

Writing Word Problems
See page 47.

Your students will put their math skills to work with this lesson. They will be encouraged to think about mathematical concepts featured in realistic fiction and use these concepts to create story problems.

The Survey Says!
See page 48.

Finally, use this activity to combine realistic fiction and graphing skills.

Theme Song Time

Objective: After hearing a song, the student will state the ways in which the song and a work of realistic fiction are related.

Standard: Uses listening and speaking strategies for different purposes

Benchmarks: Listens in order to understand topic, purpose, and perspective in spoken texts

Uses strategies to enhance listening comprehension

Skill Development: Forming inferences, listening skills

Organization: Whole-class activity

Materials

- CDs of various songs
- CD player
- copies of song lyrics

Procedure

1. Select a song that relates to the realistic fiction the class is reading. Suggested songs and related realistic fiction are included in the chart below.

Realistic Fiction	Related Song
Stone Fox by John Reynolds Gardiner	"Go the Distance." 1997. Disney Music.
Sarah, Plain and Tall by Patricia MacLachlan	"A Whole New World," 1992. Disney Music.
Anne of Green Gables by Lucy Maud Montgomery	"Part of that World," 1989. Disney Music.
Bridge to Terabitha by Katherine Paterson	"Circle of Life," 1994. Disney Music.
Jacob Have I Loved by Katherine Paterson	"Reflection," 1998. Disney Music.
The Secret School by Avi	"I Believe I Can Fly," 1996. Zomba Recording Co.

2. Tell the students that you are going to play a song that relates to the realistic fiction story they have been reading.

3. Distribute copies of the song lyrics to the students.

4. Ask the students to follow along with the lyrics as you play the song. Ask the students to think about the ways in which the song relates to the realistic fiction.

5. After playing the song, ask your students how this song relates to the realistic fiction. Did the song express the feelings of the main character? Did the song and the realistic fiction share the same setting?

6. Ask your students to name other songs that relate to the realistic fiction story.

Is That True?

Objective: The student will use reference materials to verify statements contained in realistic fiction selections.

Standard: Uses reading skills and strategies to understand and interpret a variety of informational texts

Benchmark: Uses new information to adjust and extend personal knowledge base

Skill Development: Research skills, critical thinking

Organization: Pairs

Materials

- student copies of "Is That True?" (page 45)
- realistic fiction stories
- science textbooks, encyclopedia, and computers with Internet access

Procedure

1. Many works of realistic fiction contain statements related to the elementary science curriculum. For example, the main characters might discuss the migration of birds, weather conditions, or the cause of a fire.

2. Select a work of realistic fiction that is related to your science curriculum. For example, read *Where the Red Fern Grows* by Wilson Rawls when your students are studying animal behavior in science. Additional suggestions are given in the table below.

Realistic Fiction with Science Related Topics

Realistic Fiction Selection	Author	Science Topic
Skylark	Patricia MacLachlan	Weather Conditions; droughts
Stone Fox	John Reynolds Gardiner	Animal Behavior; weather conditions in Alaska
Island of the Blue Dolphins	Scott O'Dell	Marine Life Island conditions
Lyddie	Katherine Paterson	Factory Conditions
The Ballad of Lucy Whipple	Karen Cushman	California Gold Rush; Ecological impact of mining

3. Distribute copies of "Is That True?" and ask each student to work with a partner.

4. Guide the students as they complete the page. Ask each pair to share their completed work with the class.

Is That True? Worksheet

Sometimes when we're reading, we ask ourselves, "Is that true?" When we read realistic fiction, we know that the story did not really happen. The author made it up! Realistic fiction is, however, based in reality. There are often many facts contained in each example of realistic fiction.

Work with a partner to find five science facts in the realistic fiction story that you have been reading. Complete the chart below.

The realistic fiction I am reading:

Science Fact	Page number	How can you verify this statement? List an Internet source or a reference book and page number.

Map it Out

> **Objective:** While reading a realistic fiction story, the student will chart the travels of the main characters.
>
> **Standard:** Gathers and uses information for research purposes
>
> **Benchmark:** Uses a variety of resource materials to gather information for research topics
>
> **Standard:** Uses viewing skills and strategies to understand and interpret visual media
>
> **Benchmark:** Understands how symbols, images, sound, and other conventions are used in visual media
>
> **Skill Development:** Map reading skills
>
> **Organization:** Whole-class activity

Materials

- maps of locations mentioned in realistic fiction

Procedure

1. Select a map that shows the location of the book you plan to discuss in class.

2. Display the map in a prominent location in the classroom. As the students are reading, ask them to locate the setting of the story on the map.

3. If your reading selection involves travel, you may wish to have students plot the journey of the main characters on the map.

4. Your students may be reading a group of novels set in different states, provinces, or countries. Ask your students to place a marker on the map for each reading selection.

Across Five April

Writing Word Problems

Objective: The student will write mathematical word problems based on the characters and events in the realistic fiction they are reading.

Standard: Uses a variety of strategies in the problem-solving process

Benchmark: Formulates a problem, determines information required to solve the problem, chooses methods for obtaining this information, and sets limits for acceptable solutions

Standard: Gathers and uses information for research purposes

Benchmark: Uses strategies to compile information into written reports or summaries

Skill Development: Sentence formation, problem solving

Organization: Whole-class activity, small groups

Materials

- realistic fiction stories

Procedure

1. Read a work of realistic fiction and discuss the mathematical concepts contained in it. Did the main characters raise money for a special cause? Did the main characters hold part-time jobs?

2. After discussing the mathematical concepts, invite the students to write word problems based on the story.

3. For an added challenge, divide the students into groups to write word problems. Each group then exchanges problems for another group to solve. The group that solves the word problem should offer feedback to the group that wrote the problem. Their feedback should include comments about the writing style and should answer questions, such as:

   Did the writers give clear directions?

   Was all of the necessary information contained in the reading selection?

   Word Problem Example:

   In *Where the Red Fern Grows*, Billy gathered berries to earn money. He was paid ten cents for each bucket of berries that he collected. Billy's goal was to earn fifty dollars. How many buckets of berries would Billy need to sell in order to earn fifty dollars?

4. This activity can provide you with an excellent opportunity to add math terms to students' math vocabulary.

The Survey Says!

Objective: The student will construct a graph based on information from a story.

Standard: Uses a variety of strategies in the problem-solving process

Benchmark: Generalizes from a pattern of observations made in particular cases, makes conjectures, and provides supporting arguments for these conjectures (i.e. uses inductive reasoning)

Standard: Gathers and uses information for research purposes

Benchmark: Gathers data for research topics from interviews (i.e. prepares and asks relevant questions, makes notes of responses, compiles responses)

Skill Development: Graph construction, interpreting graphs

Organization: Whole-class activity, small groups

Materials

- realistic fiction stories

Procedure

1. Ask the students to form survey questions related to the realistic fiction the class has read. Possible questions include:
   - Which did you prefer, the novel or the film version of the story?
   - Who was your favorite character in the novel?

2. Instruct each student to conduct a survey by posing their questions to their classmates.

3. Have each student construct a graph to show the results of the survey.

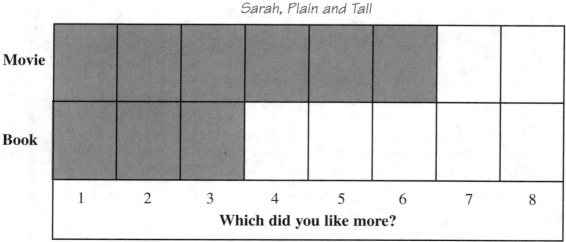

Sarah, Plain and Tall

Closure Activities

The activities in this section can be used after students have finished reading realistic fiction stories. These activities can bring closure to a unit and help students reflect on the books they have read.

Achieving a Goal and Ladder to Success
See page 50.

Your students will identify the hero or heroine in a story, discuss the ways this character worked toward goal(s), and reflect on how these efforts might inspire their own achievements.

Create a Book Jacket and Create a Bookmark
See page 54.

These activities allow your students to reflect on the plot of a story and create projects that feature book summaries and illustrations.

Design a Movie Poster and Create a Movie Storyboard
See page 57.

These activities give your students a creative outlet for retelling the events of a realistic fiction story.

Act it Out!
See page 60.

Your students display their knowledge of realistic fiction stories by entering the spotlight to perform portions of the books they've read.

Achieving a Goal

Objectives: The student will identify goals.

The student will list steps he or she can take to achieve goals.

Standard: Uses reading skills and strategies to understand and interpret a variety of literary texts

Benchmark: Understands elements of character development (i.e. character traits and motivations; interactions with other characters)

Standard: Uses the general skills and strategies of the writing process

Benchmark: Writes compositions that address problems/solutions

Skill Development: Writing skills

Organization: Whole-class or independent work

Materials

- realistic fiction stories
- student copies of "Achieving a Goal" (page 51)

Procedure

1. Use this activity after the class has read an example of realistic fiction in which the main character finds success through hard work. The *Secret School* by Avi, *Stone Fox* by John Reynolds Gardiner, and *Where the Red Fern Grows* by Wilson Rawls are examples of realistic fiction that fit this description.

2. This activity will give you an opportunity to introduce a new term, *protagonist*. A protagonist is the main character in a narrative or drama. The protagonist is the hero or heroine in a story.

3. Lead the class in a discussion about the goals of the protagonist and the ways in which he or she achieved those goals.

4. Discuss the importance of setting goals and ask the students to think about their own goals. They may consider academic goals, such as making the honor roll or improving their report card grades. They may be interested in sports and would like to set goals for sporting achievements. They might also be involved in scouting activities and could set goals for earning badges.

5. Distribute copies of "Achieving a Goal" and guide students in completing the tasks. Provide time for them to discuss their goals with their classmates.

Achieving a Goal Worksheet

The plot in a realistic fiction story often revolves around the main character (the protagonist) achieving a goal. In *The Secret School*, fourteen-year-old Ida Bidson became a teacher to keep her town's only school open. *Stone Fox* is the story of a young boy determined to help his grandfather save the family farm.

Select a realistic fiction story in which the protagonist pursues and achieves a goal. Complete the tasks below.

Realistic Fiction Story: _____

Author: _____

Copyright Date: _____

Protagonist: _____

What dream did the protagonist pursue?

_____

Did anyone help the protagonist accomplish his or her goal? Who helped?

_____

What steps did the protagonist take to achieve this goal?

_____

_____

_____

Realistic fiction can show us that it is possible to achieve our goals with hard work and persistence. Set a goal for yourself.

Goal: _____

What steps will you take to achieve your goal?

_____

_____

_____

Will you ask anyone to help you achieve your goal? If yes, identify the people you will ask to help you.

_____

_____

_____

Ladder to Success

Objective: After reading a realistic fiction story, the student will list the steps the protagonist took to achieve his or her goals.

Standard: Uses reading skills and strategies to understand and interpret a variety of literary texts

Benchmark: Understands elements of character development (i.e., character traits and motivations, interactions with other characters)

Standard: Uses the general skills and strategies of the writing process

Benchmark: Writes compositions that address problems/solutions

Skill Development: Writing skills

Organization: Whole-class or independent work

Materials

- realistic fiction stories
- student copies of "Ladder to Success" (page 53)
- paper

Procedure

1. Use this activity as a follow-up to the previous lesson, "Achieving a Goal."

2. Review with the students the term protagonist.

3. Remind them that a protagonist is the main character in a narrative or drama. The protagonist is the hero or heroine of the story.

4. Lead the class in a discussion about the goals set by a particular protagonist and the ways he or she achieved those goals.

5. Distribute copies of "Ladder to Success." Guide the students in completing the page.

6. After completing the page, instruct each student to use a separate sheet of paper to write a paragraph. The paragraph should address the goal set by the main character, the steps the main character took to achieve that goal, and the results.

Ladder to Success *(cont.)*

The plot in a realistic fiction story often revolves around the main character (the protagonist) achieving a goal. Select a realistic fiction story in which the protagonist pursues and fulfills a goal. Complete the information required on the "Ladder to Success." Write a paragraph containing the information.

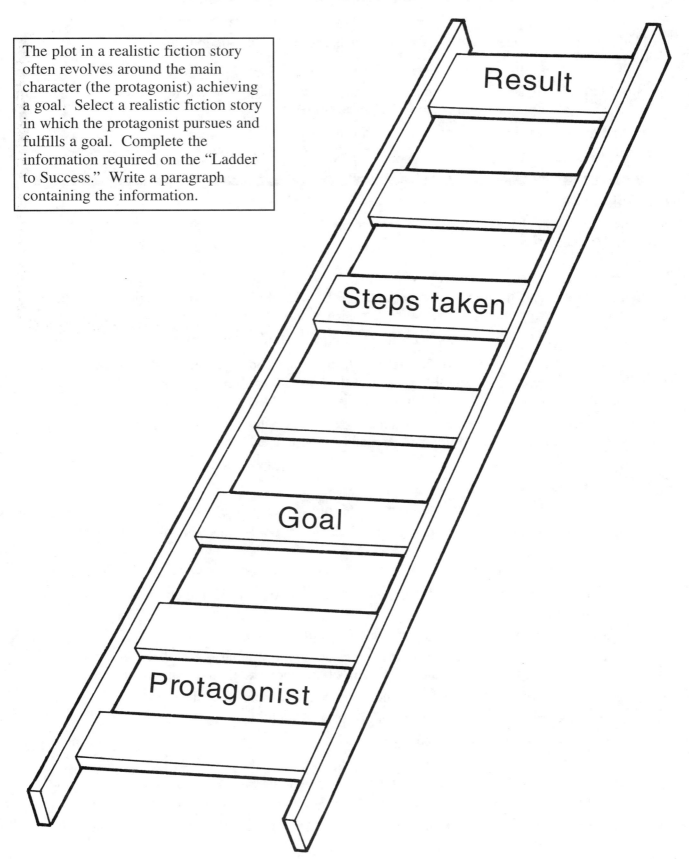

Result

Steps taken

Goal

Protagonist

Create a Book Jacket

Objective: The student will create a book jacket for a realistic fiction story.

Standard: Uses the general skills and strategies of the reading process

Benchmark: Reflects on what has been learned after reading and formulates ideas, opinions, and personal responses to text

Skill Development: Main idea, writing a summary

Organization: Whole-class or independent work

Materials:

- books with book jackets
- drawing paper
- crayons
- markers
- paper grocery bags
- scissors

Procedure:

1. Invite your students to examine the book jackets of several of their favorite books. Book jackets usually have an appealing picture on the front cover and an intriguing summary on the back.

2. Challenge each of your students to create a book jacket for a realistic fiction story.

3. Provide time for the students to prepare first drafts of their book jackets on drawing paper. Each draft should include a picture for the cover of the book jacket and a summary for the back of the book jacket. The summary should motivate others to read the story.

4. Assist the students in making book jackets from grocery bags to fit the books they have chosen from the school or classroom library. To make the book jacket:

   — Open a grocery bag. Cut the flat bottom portion from the bag.

   — Cut out one side of the bag.

   — Place the book to be covered in the center of the rectangular sheet.

   — Fold down the top portion of the rectangular sheet until it meets the top of the book. Crease along the fold line.

   — Place the top of the book on the top fold line.

   — Fold the bottom portion of the rectangular sheet until it meets the bottom of the book to be covered.

   — Crease along the fold line. Place the bottom of the book on the bottom fold line.

   — Place the book to be covered in the center of the rectangular sheet. The top of the book should touch the top fold and the bottom of the book should touch the bottom fold.

   — Cover the front of the book with the excess paper to the left of the book.

   — Fold the excess paper over the front of the book and tuck in the ends.

   — Close the book. Cover the back of the book with the excess paper to the right of the book. Tuck in the ends and secure.

5. After making the book jacket, have each student draw a picture and write the book's title and author on the cover. The student should write the summary on the back of the book jacket.

6. Challenge your students to read and make book jackets for all of the books in your classroom library by the end of the school year.

54

Create a Bookmark

Objective: The student will create a bookmark for a realistic fiction story.

Standard: Uses the general skills and strategies of the reading process

Benchmark: Reflects on what has been learned after reading and formulates ideas, opinions, and personal responses to text

Skill Development: Main idea

Organization: Whole-class activity, independent work

Materials

- sample bookmarks
- student copies of "Create a Bookmark" (page 56)
- crayons
- markers

Procedure

1. Encourage your students to combine their enjoyment of books and their artistic talents to create unique bookmarks. Students will have the opportunity to reflect on the book and think about the characters and events that make the book memorable.

2. Bring a variety of bookmarks to class to display for your students. Tell the class that bookmarks are often created to commemorate special events or to motivate people to read new books.

3. Tell the students that they will create bookmarks to inspire their classmates to read works of realistic fiction.

4. Ask each student to select a work of realistic fiction. (You may wish to have the students select from a list of books contained in your classroom library or the school library.)

5. Distribute student copies of "Create a Bookmark." Read and discuss the directions with your students. (If desired, copy the page on heavy paper to create sturdy bookmarks.)

6. Display the completed bookmarks in a basket near your classroom library or in the school library. Encourage students to select bookmarks each time they go to the library.

Create a Bookmark Worksheet

Ask yourself the following questions.

- What is your favorite book?
- Why is it your favorite book?
- Does the book have great pictures or funny phrases?

Directions:

1. Select a work of realistic fiction.

2. Use boxes on this page to create a bookmark related to the story. Your bookmark will be given to other students. Be sure that your bookmark is designed to grab students' attention and motivate them to read the book.

3. Draw a picture to represent the realistic fiction story. Write on the bookmark a memorable phrase or funny expression from the book.

4. When you have finished the bookmark, cut it out and give it to your teacher to display.

Title

Title

Design a Movie Poster

Objective: The student will create a poster related to a realistic fiction story.

Standard: Understands the characteristics and components of media

Benchmark: Understands aspects of media production and distribution

Standard: Uses the general skills and strategies of the reading process

Benchmark: Reflects on what has been learned after reading and formulates ideas, opinions, and personal responses to text

Skill Development: Main idea, writing headlines

Organization: Whole-class activity, pairs, or independent work

Materials

- movie posters or newspaper movie ads
- drawing paper
- crayons
- markers

Procedure

1. Bring movie posters or movie ads from the newspaper to the classroom to use as examples. You may be able to obtain posters for your classroom by speaking to the manager of a local movie theater.

2. Instruct your students to examine the movie posters.

   - What words are used to entice an audience?
   - How do the pictures reflect the main idea of the film?
   - What gets the most emphasis on the poster?

3. Ask your students to work in pairs or independently to create posters for realistic fiction stories.

4. Display the completed posters in the classroom, school library, or in the hallway to motivate other students to read the books.

Create a Movie Storyboard

Objective: The student will draw pictures and write captions to show the sequence of a realistic fiction story.

Standard: Uses the general skills and strategies of the reading process

Benchmark: Represents concrete information (i.e., people, places, things, events) as explicit mental pictures

Skill Development: Main idea, sentence construction

Organization: Whole-class activity or independent work

Materials
- comic strips from the newspaper
- student copies of "Create a Movie Storyboard" Worksheet (page 59)
- drawing paper

Procedure

1. Discuss the concept of a movie storyboard with your class.

2. Tell students that a storyboard uses pictures to tell a story. Film makers use storyboards to outline major events in the stories they wish to tell. If desired, display for the students a book, such as *Disney's Mulan: Special Collector's Edition*, which shows the ways filmmakers create storyboards to plan their projects.

3. Bring comic strips to class to further explain the concept of storyboards. Use the comic strips to explain that a story can be told sequentially in pictures.

4. Tell the students that they will each have the opportunity to create a storyboard for the realistic fiction story the class is currently reading. Distribute student copies of "Create a Storyboard" and guide the students in following the directions.

Create a Movie Storyboard Worksheet

Many movies are based on popular realistic fiction books. Filmmakers begin their projects by creating storyboards. A storyboard looks like a cartoon strip and contains pictures of the main events in sequence.

Create a storyboard for a realistic fiction book you have recently read. Your storyboard should tell the story in six pictures.

Directions:

1. The first picture should set the stage for the story. Draw a picture that shows the setting and the main character(s).

2. Tell the story. Draw four pictures to show what happens in the middle of the story.

3. Draw a picture that shows the conclusion of the story.

4. Write a caption below each picture.

Act It Out!

Objective: The student will dramatize a scene from a realistic fiction story.

Standard: Uses listening and speaking strategies for different purposes

Benchmark: Makes oral presentations to the class

Skill Development: Speaking skills, understanding story sequence

Organization: Small groups

Materials

- index cards
- realistic fiction books
- props

Procedure

1. Choose exciting events from a familiar realistic fiction book for the students to dramatize.

2. Write each event on an index card.

3. Divide the students into small groups.

4. Ask each group to select a card.

5. Provide time for each group to discuss the event they have chosen. The students can refer to the realistic fiction book to reread the part that they plan to dramatize.

6. Provide props to assist the students in dramatizing their scenes.

7. In their groups, have the students reflect on their chosen event and think about how the characters reacted. What did they say? What did they do? Ask the groups to plan their reenactments. Allow them to create their own dialogue to fit the scene.

8. Allow the students time to rehearse.

9. Schedule a time for each group to perform for their classmates.

Integrating Technology

In this section, you'll find a wealth of ideas for integrating technology into your language arts program. (As with any instructional material, it is essential for you to preview DVDs, videos, and television programs to ensure appropriate content.)

Internet Ideas

See page 62.

The Internet can link readers to authors and resources that will enhance understanding and enjoyment of realistic fiction stories. For ideas integrating Internet activities into realistic fiction have students e-mail authors or literary penpals. They may also use the Internet to better research the setting of the story or visit publisher's Web sites.

DVDs, Videotape, and TV Programs

See page 63.

DVDs, videotapes, and television programs of realistic fiction stories can enhance the literary experience. Students can benefit by watching and discussing a videotape, DVD, or television program based on a realistic fiction book that they have not yet read or they can read a selection and then view the program afterwards.

When using a videotape, television program, or DVD of a realistic fiction book, it is not always necessary to show the entire program. You might want to have the students read several chapters and then watch and discuss those portions of the videotape. The class can then proceed in this manner until they have watched the entire program. You may wish to show only those scenes that clarify a topic of class discussion.

Internet Ideas

The Internet can link readers to authors and resources that will enhance understanding and enjoyment of realistic fiction stories. Use the ideas below to guide students in using Internet resources.

E-mail the Author

E-mail can enable readers to communicate with their favorite authors. Find authors' e-mail addresses by visiting the publisher's Web site for links to authors. Another way is by entering the author's name in a search engine. This can lead to various links related to the author, publisher, and literature-related Web sites.

Guidelines for e-mails to an author:

1. Determine the purpose before composing an e-mail message. Is this an e-mail to congratulate the author on another terrific book or do you have specific questions?

2. Form appropriate questions for the author. To write a question, reflect upon the message of the novel and consider the motivations of the main characters. This will develop higher level thinking skills.

3. Coordinate a class response. When the entire class is reading the same novel, you can send one message rather than individual messages from every student. You might wish to form a student committee to gather questions from classmates and compose the message to the author.

4. Take time to compose a message. Use pencil and paper or a word processing program to write a rough draft of the e-mail message. An e-mail message to an author deserves the same attention as a traditional letter.

E-mail Literary Penpals

Invite your students to discuss their favorite books with an e-mail penpal. Coordinate your study of realistic fiction with a teacher of a similar grade level in your school district. When your classes are reading the same novel or novels by the same author, you can match your students for e-mail discussions. Instruct your students to answer these questions in their first messages to penpals:

1. What part of the book did you like best?

2. Who was your favorite character?

3. Did the book end the way you thought it would end?

In future correspondence, the penpals could make recommendations for interesting independent reading and they could discuss projects they complete in response to their reading.

Research the Setting

Students develop better understanding of a reading selection when they learn more about the setting. Encourage students to use the Internet to research the time and place where a story occurs.

1. If the story takes place in a major city such as New York, Chicago, or Philadelphia, the students can visit the tourism Web sites for those cities. These Web sites often provide information on sites and events mentioned in the realistic fiction selections. For example, in the novel *Crash*, 7th grade athlete Crash Coogan, dreams of running in the Penn Relays. The Penn Relays are a respected track meet held in Philadelphia, Pennsylvania each year. Students reading *Crash* could go to the Philadelphia Web site to learn more about the Penn Relays and Franklin Field where the relays are held.

Internet Ideas *(cont.)*

2. Students can use weather related Web sites to find the temperature and weather conditions in the city where the story occurs.

3. When reading historical fiction, students can enter a major historical event such as the Boston Tea Party in an Internet search engine. Students will see the many possibilities available for research.

Visit the Publisher's Web Site

Major publishers often have Web sites containing biographical information about authors, information on related books, and games and activities related to the books. Visit these Web sites and select appropriate activities.

Visit the Read-Write-Think Web site (http://www.readwritethink.org)

Read-Write-Think is a partnership between the International Reading Association (IRA), the National Council of Teachers of English (NCTE) and the Marco Polo Education Foundation. The Read-Write-Think Web site contains standards-based lesson plans which teachers can use to help students explore realistic fiction and develop critical literacy skills.

After selecting appropriate lessons, direct students to Interactive tools on the Read-Write-Think Web site. Students can complete story maps, play word games, and write their own books using tools found on this Web site.

DVDs, Videotapes, and TV Programs

Here are suggestions for using DVDs, videotapes, and television programs in the realistic fiction unit.

Main Idea

Students truly understand a reading selection when they can state the main idea using only a few sentences. You can teach your students to summarize by watching and discussing realistic programs with them.

Invite students to watch a realistic fiction DVD, videotape, or television program. After watching the program, guide students toward stating the main idea in only three or four sentences. List their responses on the chalkboard. Then compare their responses with the program description on the cover of the DVD, videocassette, or in the television program guide. Students can use the television program guide or cover of the DVD or videocassette to determine whether they have identified the main idea of the program.

Captioned Programming

Your students can reap many benefits from watching captioned programming. They will increase their sight vocabulary by seeing and hearing new words presented in context. They will develop fluency in their oral reading as they read the captions and hear the actors speak the words clearly with appropriate expression.

Choose a DVD, videotape, or television program of a realistic fiction story that the students have not yet read. Introduce the program as you would a traditional reading selection. Play the program with sound and with captions. Give the students time to enjoy the film and read the captions silently as the film plays. In the next class session invite the students to read the captions orally as the film plays.

DVDs, Videotapes, and TV Programs *(cont.)*

Compare and Contrast

Invite the students to watch a film of a realistic fiction story with which they are familiar. After watching the film, ask the students to compare it to the written work.

—Did the film use the same point of view as the written work?

—Would you recommend that a person watch the movie first and then read the book or vise versa? Why?

—Did the effects used in the film enhance or take away from your enjoyment of the story?

—Do you think the film received an appropriate rating? (This would give the teacher an opportunity to discuss the film rating system with the class.)

Captioned Summary

When watching a captioned program, hit the pause button to freeze the captions on the screen. This will give the class the opportunity to read and discuss the captions at critical points in the film.

Writing Captions

Encourage your students to write their own captions for a film. If you regularly show captioned films in class, your students will become familiar with the style in which captions are presented.

Show a five- to ten-minute segment of a realistic fiction film that the students have already seen in its entirety. Show the segment again without the sound. As a class, write new captions for the five- to ten-minute film segment. This activity will require the students to focus on the characters and setting. Your students will have to write dialogue appropriate for the characters. They will need to think about the main idea as they write.

After you have written captions for the initial five- to ten-minute segment, divide the students into groups to write captions for additional five-minute film segments. Have groups read captions aloud.

Audience Reaction

A moviemaker often tests his or her product on an audience before releasing a film to the general public. Invite your students to participate in similar research.

Read a realistic fiction story with your class and show the film version of it. By reading, watching, and discussing the story in class, your students should become very familiar with it. Then invite your students to share this story with others.

Tell the class that you would like to give them an opportunity to learn how others feel about this story. Invite a class of a similar grade level to come to your classroom to view the film. Your students, who have already read the book and seen the film, should be present in the classroom to act as observers. (Distribute copies of "Audience Reaction Survey" on page 65 to guide this activity.) Have your students look for the following:

—Did the audience laugh at appropriate times?

—Did the audience seem to pay attention or did they fidget in their seats?

—Did the audience understand the story without having to read the book?

When the film ends, pair each of your students with one of the visitors. Ask your students to interview their partners to assess their understanding of the film. After the visitors leave your room, have your students meet to discuss their notes.

Audience Reaction Survey

When filmmakers want to know if a new movie will be a hit, they play the movie for a test audience. A test audience is a group of volunteers who watch a new film. As the test audience watches the film, the filmmakers observe the audience to see whether they laugh at the jokes, cry during the sad scenes, and cheer for the hero. If the test audience likes the film, it will probably be a hit.

After watching a film in class, invite another class to come to your room to watch it. The visiting class will be your test audience. Use this page to take notes as your test audience watches the film.

Film Title: _____

Write one sentence to state the main idea of the film.

_____

Identify the test audience: _____

_____

Number of students _____

Grade _____

Answer yes or no to the following questions:

1. Did the audience seem to pay attention during the film? _____

2. Did members of the audience talk to their friends during the film? _____

3. Did the audience laugh during funny parts of the film? _____

4. Did the audience seem to understand the film? _____

5. Write a paragraph to state whether the test audience liked or did not like the film.

_____

_____

_____

_____

_____

_____

_____

_____

Unit Management

This section provides information and activities that will help you tie your realistic fiction unit together.

Home/School Connection
See page 67.

Everyone has a busy schedule yet we make time for the activities that matter most. Encourage parents to monitor and guide their children's reading by participating in the following activities.

Reading Log
See page 68.

A reading log is provided to help you and your students organize work. Because you are accountable to parents, principals, and the community, you must have records to show that you have guided your students toward meeting the standards. The reading log will show that the students have participated in a structured reading program.

Thematic Teaching
See page 71.

Students are able to make connections and understand related concepts when learning is linked across subject areas. A social studies class, for example, may be learning about the Revolutionary War. During the social studies period these students might read a nonfiction trade book such as *And Then What Happened, Paul Revere?* by Jean Fritz. Reinforce a social studies lesson by asking the students to read a related realistic fiction story, such as *Johnny Tremain* by Esther Forbes. Longfellow's narrative poem, "Paul Revere's Ride," would give students an additional opportunity to learn about Paul Revere and to connect lessons across disciplines.

The thematic chart will assist you in identifying realistic fiction stories and poems that correspond with specific themes.

Organizing for Instruction
See page 74.

The books and students are waiting. Now you must determine the best ways to guide students as they read and respond to literature. There are many ways to organize the classroom for literacy instruction. The instructional formats of guided reading, paired reading/buddy reading, independent reading, and literature circles are described in this section.

Home/School Connection

Parent/Child Book Club

Have a parent/child book club one evening each month. Parents and children would have one month to read a popular realistic fiction story together. On the appointed night, the group discusses the book and its relevance to their lives. You may choose to lead the first session for the group. Encourage parents and students to volunteer to lead future meetings.

Book Swap

Invite students to bring books they have finished reading for a classroom or school-wide book swap. Group the books attractively on tables. If you are having a book swap in one classroom, you might group the books by genre. For a school-wide book swap, you may wish to group the books by grade level. Give each child one ticket for every book he or she donated to the swap. Then invite the children to examine the books on the tables and trade their tickets for books.

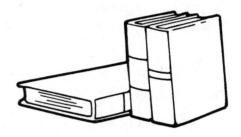

Parents may also wish to participate in a book swap as well. Invite them to bring books they have finished reading to a PTA meeting or Back to School Night. Group the books by genres and allow time for the participants to examine the books. Give the adults a ticket for each book they donated and allow them to exchange the tickets for books.

Family Movie Night

You may have the good fortune of acquiring a classroom library of videotapes and DVDs of the realistic fiction books your students are reading in class. Encourage families to borrow these programs from your classroom library. This will enable parents to discuss the reading selections with their children and help to improve home/school communication. (If you do not own copies of the necessary videotapes or DVDs, provide parents with a list of the books you are reading in class. Families can borrow the videotapes and DVDs from a public library or rent them from a local movie store.)

Listen While You Drive

Families may wish to obtain audio tapes or cds of realistic fiction books. Encourage families to play the tapes or cds on road trips or while doing the dinner dishes at home. Audio tapes or cds can often be borrowed from public libraries or purchased in bookstores.

Family Read Aloud

Encourage families to read realistic fiction stories aloud. Have parents and children take turns reading while in the car, washing the dinner dishes, or completing other household chores.

Reading Log

The reading log is beneficial for students because it helps them to organize their work. It gives them a place to write questions they would like to ask in class. It also requires them to write a main idea to summarize each chapter.

To Use the Reading Log:

Your students will need one reading log for each book they read.

1. Distribute the reading logs on the first day that you assign a book to be read.

2. On the reading log, have each student write his or her name and the title and author of the book being read.

3. You will need to model the use of the reading log. Make a copy of the reading log (page 70) on the chalkboard and fill in the chart as you work with your students.

4. Select a book. Discuss the title with the class and ask them to predict what the book will be about. Read the first chapter aloud to the class.

5. As you are reading aloud, pause periodically to discuss the chapter. Write your questions in the column labeled "Questions and Ideas to Discuss in Class." At this point, simply pose the questions for the students to consider. Do not spend time discussing the questions. An extended discussion period may detract from the students' enjoyment of the story.

6. After you have finished reading the first chapter, tell the class that they need to summarize the chapter so they will remember it the next day. Discuss the main characters and events of the chapter with your students. Working together, compose one sentence to state the main idea of the chapter.

7. By reading and discussing the first chapter, you have demonstrated the use of the reading log for your students. You may want to read and discuss chapter 2, in a similar manner, if you think your students need additional practice. If you feel your students are ready to work independently, ask them to read the next chapter and complete that section of the reading log.

Sample Reading Log
<u>Lyddie</u>
by Katherine Paterson

Chapter	Questions and Ideas to Discuss in Class	Main Idea
Chapter 1	Why did Lyddie's father leave the family? Why didn't Lyddie like her Aunt Clarissa? What did Lyddie's mother mean when she talked about going to the poor farm?	Lyddie and her brother Charles tried to save the family farm.
Chapter 2	What could Lyddie and Charles do with the money they earned by selling the calf? Why didn't Lyddie and Charles just run away?	Lyddie and Charles sold their calf and left the farm.
Chapter 3	Will Lyddie run away from the tavern to work in the mills?	Lyddie began her work at the tavern.

Student Reading Log

Book Title _____

Author _____

Write notes as you read to help you remember important details from each chapter. Use this reading log to write questions you want to ask your teacher and classmates, write notes about the chapter, and record main ideas.

1. As you are reading, write questions and/or ideas that occur to you. Write questions and ideas for chapter 1 in the first row, questions and ideas for chapter 2 in the second row, etc. You can discuss these questions and ideas with your teacher and classmates during a class discussion period.

2. When you have finished reading a chapter, write one sentence to state the main idea of that chapter.

Chapter	Questions and Ideas to Discuss in Class	Main Idea

Thematic Teaching

The chart below will help you find narrative poems and nonfiction titles to complement the realistic fiction the class is reading.

Theme	Narrative Poem	Realistic Fiction	Nonfiction
Abraham Lincoln	"O Captain! My Captain!" by Walt Whitman	*With Every Drop of Blood* by J.L. Collier & C. Collier. Delacorte Press, 1992	*Lincoln: A Photobiography* by Russell Freedman. Clarion Books, 1987
Adoption	Lady Clare by Alfred Lord Tennyson	*Karen's Sister* by Elisabet McHugh Greenwillow, 1983	*How It Feels to be Adopted* by Jill Krementz Knopf, 1982
American Revolution	"Paul Revere's Ride" by Henry Wadsworth Longfellow	*Johnny Tremain* by Esther Forbes. Houghton-Mifflin, 1943	*And Then What Happened, Paul Revere?* by Jean Fritz. Coward-McCann, 1973
American Revolution (Role of Women)	"Molly Pitcher" by Kate Brownlee Sherwood	*Sarah Bishop* by Scott O'Dell. Houghton-Mifflin, 1980	*Molly Pitcher, Young Patriot* by Augusta Stevenson. Aladdin Library, 1986
Baseball	"Casey at the Bat" by Ernest Lawrence Thayer	*Catcher with a Glass Arm* by Matt Christopher. Little Brown & Co., 1991	*Like Father, Like Son: Baseball's Major League Families* by Sarah Gardiner. White, Scholastic, 1993
Bears	"The Lady and the Bear" by Theodore Roethke	*Beardance* by Will Hobbs. Atheneum, 1993	*The Moon of the Bears* by Jean Craighead George. HarperCollins, 1993
Cats	"The Cats of Kilkenny" and Old Possum's Book of Practical Cats by T.S.Eliot Harcourt, 1982 (1939)	*A Question of Trust* by Marion Dane Bauer Scholastic, 1994	*The True or False Book of Cats* by Patricia Lauber National Geographic, 1998
Christmas	"A Visit form St. Nicholas" by Clement Clarke Moore	*The Christmas Doll* by Elvira Woodruff. Scholastic, 2000	*The Doubleday Christmas Treasury* compiled by Jane Olliver. Doubleday & Co., 1986
Civil War	"Barbara Frietchie" by John Greenleaf Whittier	*Across Five Aprils* by Irene Hunt. Follet, 1964	*Behind the Blue and Gray: The Soldier's Life in the Civil War* by Delia Ray. Dutton, 1991
Courage	"The Tale of Custard the Dragon" by Ogden Nash	*The Courage of Sarah Noble* by Alice Daigliesh Scribner's Sons, 1954	*Profiles in Courage for Our Time* by Caroline Kennedy (editor) Hyperion, 2002
Deafness	"There Was a Child Went Forth" by Walt Whitman	*The Gift of the Girl Who Couldn't Hear* by Susan Shreve Tambourine, 1991	*A Show of Hands: Say It In Sign Language* by Linda Bourke and Mary Beth Sullivan with Susan Regan Addison, 1980

Thematic Teaching *(cont.)*

Theme	Narrative Poem	Realistic Fiction	Nonfiction
Dogs	"My Dog, Tray" by Thomas Campbell	*Where the Red Fern Grows* by Wilson Rawls. Doubleday, 1961	*Dogs, All About Them* by Alvin & Virginia Silverstein Lothrop. Lee & Shepard Books, 1986
Elderly	"Father William" by Lewis Carroll	*Rules of the Road* by Joan Bauer Putnam's, 1998	*If I Live to Be 100: Lessons from the Centenarians* by Neenah Ellis Crown Publishing, 2002
Elephants	"The Blind Men and the Elephant" by John Godfrey Saxe	*The Elephant's Bathtub: Wonder Tales from the Far East* by Frances Carpenter. Doubleday & Co., 1962	*Jane Goodall's Animal World: Elephants* by Miriam Schlein. Atheneum, 1990
Employment/Job Opportunities	"The Village Blacksmith" by Henry Wadsworth Longfellow	*Is Anybody There?* by Eve Bunting Harper, 1988	*Cesar Chavez* by Bruce W. Conord Chelsea, 1992
Families/ Fathers	"Daddy Fell into the Pond" by Alfred Noyes	*The Robbers* by Nina Bawden Lothrop, 1979	*Who Were the Founding Fathers?: Two Hundred Years of Reinventing American History* by Steven H. Jaffe Holt, 1996
Families/ Mothers	"Somebody's Mother" Anonymous	*Karen and Vicki* by Elisabet McHugh Greenwillow, 1989	*Growing Up Adopted* by Maxine B. Rosenberg Bradbury, 1989
Farming	"The Day No One Came to the Peanut Picker" by Jimmy Carter	*Night Cry* by Phyllis Reynolds Naylor. Atheneum, 1984	*Portrait of a Farm Family* by Raymond Bial. Houghton, 1995
Fish	"The Fish" by Elizabeth Bishop	*Armien's Fishing Trip* by Catherine Stock Morrow, 1990	*Beneath the Sea in 3-D* by Mark Blum Chronicle, 1997
Horses	"The Runaway" by Robert Frost	*The Black Stallion* by Walter Farley. Random, 1941	*Once Upon a Horse: A History of Horses and How They Shaped Our History* by Suzanne Jurmain. Lothrop, 1989
Jealousy	"The Fox and the Grapes" by Joseph Lauren	*Jacob Have I Loved* by Katherine Paterson Crowell, 1980	*I Have Feelings* by Terry Berger, Photos by Howard I. Spivak Human Science, 1971
Learning Disabilities	"Life Doesn't Frighten Me" by Maya Angelou	*Probably Still Nick Swansen* by Virginia Euwer Wolff Holt, 1988	*Author: A True Story* by Helen Lester Houghton, 1997

Thematic Teaching *(cont.)*

Theme	Narrative Poem	Realistic Fiction	Nonfiction
Music	"A Musical Instrument" by Elizabeth Barrett Browning	*The Mozart Season* by Virginia Euwer Wolff Holt, 1991	*A Pianist's Debut: Preparing for the Concert Stage* by Barbara Beirne Carolrhoda, 1990
Journey	"Landing of the Pilgrim Fathers" by Felicia Hemans	*By the Great Horn Spoon!* by Sid Fleischman Little Brown, 1963	*To Space and Back* by Sally Ride and Susan Okie Lothrop, 1986
Native Americans	"Hiawatha" by Henry Wadsworth Longfellow	*Courage of Sarah Noble* by Alice Dalgliesh Schribner's Sons, 1954	*Pocahontas* by Catherine Iannone, Chelsea Juniors, 1996
Patriotism	"The Little Black-Eyed Rebel" by Will Carleton	*Shadow of the Dragon* by Sherry Garland Harcourt Brace, 1993 (1961)	*John F. Kennedy* by Judie Mills Watts, 1988
Schools	"Sick" by Shel Silverstein	*Nothing But the Truth: A Documentary Novel* by Avi Orchard, 1991	*A One-Room School* by Bobbie Kalman Crabtree, 1994
Shipwrecks	"The Wreck of the Hesperus" by Henry Wadsworth Longfellow	*The Wreckers* by Ian Lawrence. Delacorte, 1998	*Shipwrecked: The True Adventures of a Japanese Boy* by Rhoda Blumberg Harper Collins, 2001
Slavery	"Harriet Tubman" by Eloise Greenfield	*Stealing Freedom* by Elisa Carbone Knopf, 1998	*Harriet Tubman and the Fight Against Slavery* by Bree Burns Chelsea House, 1992
Thanksgiving	"Landing of the Pilgrim Fathers" by Felicia Hemans	*Standard at Plimoth Plantation 1626* by Gary Bowen Harper, 1994	*The First Thanksgiving Feast* by Joan Anderson Clarion, 1984
Titanic	"The Great Ship" by Mike Kavanaugh	*Titanic Crossing* by Barbara Williams. Dial Books, 1995	*Exploring the Titanic* by Robert Ballard. Madison Publishing, 1988
Urban/Suburban Living	"The City Mouse and the Garden Mouse" by Christina Georgina Rossetti	*The Star Fisher* by Laurence Yep Morrow, 1991	*Homeless* by Bernard Wolf Orchard, 1995

Organizing for Instruction

Guided Reading

Guided Reading can take place with whole-class or small group instruction. In Guided Reading, the teacher introduces the selection and sets a purpose for reading. The teacher divides the reading selection into segments. When assigning a segment, the teacher assigns a task such as, "Read Chapter 1 to learn why Billy left school early on Monday." The students read the segment silently and then discuss it with the teacher. Instruction proceeds in this manner until the entire selection has been read. The class may complete a culminating activity such as a book report or an art project related to the story.

Steps in a Guided Reading Lesson

1. *Introduce*

   Build motivation by discussing the selection with the students. Discuss the author, the setting for the selection, and the problems confronting the main characters. Prepare the students for reading by introducing vocabulary that is essential for understanding the story.

2. *Read*

   Set a purpose and guide the students as they read the selection. For example tell the students, "Read chapter one to learn why Ellen and Annemarie ran away from the soldiers." The students should read the segment silently and then discuss it with the teacher. Ask students to form predictions about upcoming sections of the book. After students have read a section, ask if their predictions were correct. Proceed in this manner until the students have read the entire selection.

3. *Respond*

   Provide opportunities for the students to respond to the text orally and in writing. Begin with a discussion of the text. As you discuss the story, guide students to form inferences about the main characters' motivations and feelings. Students can use reading logs to write a response to their reading.

4. *Apply*

   Teach skills and strategies related to the reading selection. Review vocabulary, help students put the main events in sequence, and guide students in stating the main idea of the selection.

Paired Reading/ Buddy Reading

Some students may be more comfortable discussing a reading selection with a partner rather than a group. In Paired Reading/Buddy Reading, students are teamed with classmates to read a selection. The team may choose to take turns reading aloud to each other or they may each read a portion silently and then meet to discuss it.

There are many ways to group students for paired reading/buddy reading. Some teachers prefer to pair students of equal reading ability. Other teachers find it beneficial to pair a strong reader with a student who struggles with reading. The stronger reader who offers support and a model of fluent reading, is able to reinforce his or her own skills by guiding a classmate.

Organizing for Instruction *(cont.)*

Choral Reading

Choral reading is a technique in which groups of students read aloud together. Although both prose and poetry can be used, teachers usually introduce choral reading with poetry. To begin a choral reading activity, select a poem and divide the class into two groups. First ask both groups to read the poem together. The ask each group to read alternating stanzas. Suggested poems for choral reading include:

"The Little Blue Engine" by Shel Silverstein

"Father William" by Lewis Carroll

"Charge of the Light Brigade" by Alfred Lord Tennyson

"O Captain! My Captain!" by Walt Whitman

"Stopping by Woods on a Snowy Evening" by Robert Frost

Choral Reading can help students develop fluent, expressive reading. It can also support struggling readers as they strive to build word recognition skills.

Sustained Silent Reading/Independent Reading

Sustained Silent Reading (SSR) is an instructional practice that demonstrates the importance of reading. During this time, you and your students are given uninterrupted time to read a story of choice.

To begin the SSR period, each student selects a book to read for enjoyment. No book reports or other assignments will be required. Tell the class that they will have uninterrupted reading time to enjoy their books. SSR periods usually last from 15 to 30 minutes. You might want to begin with a brief period (15 minutes) early in the school year and increase the time as the students grow in maturity and familiarity with the routine.

To model the significance and enjoyment of reading, it is essential for everyone (students, teachers, visitors, assistants, etc.) in the classroom to participate in the Sustained Silent Reading.

Literature Circles

Literature Circles provide an opportunity for students to meet with friends to discuss good books. This technique transforms reading into a social activity.

Purposes of Literature Circles

—Students take responsibility for their reading.

—Students learn to work with classmates to complete tasks.

—Students have an opportunity to discuss good books with friends.

Procedure

1. To begin using Literature Circles in your classroom, select three to five books with a common theme. Introduce each book by showing it to the class and giving a quick teaser or motivating preview. Place copies of the books in a learning center so students can examine them and select the book they would like to read.

2. Ask students to form groups based on the books they have chosen. Groups should have five to seven members.

Organizing for Instruction *(cont.)*

3. Each student should be prepared to assume a role/responsibility in the group. Suggested roles include:

   Chairperson: The chairperson assumes leadership for the group and coordinates activities.

   Timekeeper: The timekeeper makes sure that the students are using the daily instructional time efficiently.

   Secretary: The secretary records notes at each meeting.

   Reporter: The reporter gives daily progress updates to the teacher

   Material Coordinator: The material coordinator takes responsibility for distributing the books and the materials necessary for completing assignments.

   Spokespersons: The spokespersons present the group's assignment to the entire class.

4. Have each group set their own timetable for reading the novel and completing the assignments by the deadline.

   Early in the school year, you may wish to give specific assignments related to each book. After the students have gained experience with literature circles, they can design their own responses to the reading selections.

   Suggested assignments/responses to the books:
   - Art project such as a poster, diorama, classroom bulletin board
   - Letter to the author
   - Reader's Theater presentation
   - Oral Report
   - Book Report
   - Literary Newsletter to be distributed in the school or community library

5. Encourage groups to meet on a regular basis to discuss their reading.

6. Instruct students to update and bring their Reading Log pages to each session of the literature circle. The students should begin the session by discussing the entries they made in the questions/idea column. The focus of the literature circle should be on the content of the novel rather than on isolated skills.

Reading Aloud

Oral reading opportunities can build a student's self-esteem and can help him or her feel comfortable with public speaking. Here are suggestions that can make oral reading a vibrant, positive experience for all students.

Memorable Messages

Rather than assigning oral reading passages, ask each student to select a paragraph that holds special meaning. Give students time to practice reading their selected paragraphs. Then ask each student to read his or her paragraph to the class.

Locating Information

Ask the students to find and read sentences in the book that answer specific questions. For example, you might ask, "Why did Jess think he could be the fastest runner in fifth grade? Find a sentence that supports your answer."

Organizing for Instruction *(cont.)*

Captioned Reading

There are many videotapes and DVDs that correspond to the realistic fiction. You may wish to play a videotape or DVD as a pre- or post-reading activity. When showing the program, use the closed-captioned feature so that students can read the captions as they watch. This will help students build sight vocabulary. The actors will serve as models of fluent oral reading.

After students have watched the videotape or DVD, play the program again without the sound. Ask the students to read the captions as an oral reading activity. This will give students an opportunity to read with expression.

Audio Books

Commercially prepared audio books (books on tape or cds) can provide excellent models of oral reading. When studying a realistic fiction book with your students, bring a commercially prepared audio tape or cd of the selection to class. Play a chapter as the students follow along. Then ask the students to divide into groups to make their own audio tapes of subsequent chapters.

Vocabulary Viewpoints

Here are suggestions for developing vocabulary as your students read realistic fiction.

Word File

Each student needs a supply of index cards and a file box. Each student should make a card for each new word encountered in the book. Each card should include the new word, a definition, and a sentence containing the word. Have students keep their file boxes on their desks to use as a spelling guide.

Word Wall

Establish a place in the classroom, such as a bulletin board or blank wall space where new words can be displayed. Each time students encounter new words in their reading, write the words on index cards and attach them to the word wall. Encourage students to refer to the word wall when adding descriptive words to their writing or when they need help spelling new words.

Morphemic Messages

Morphemes are the smallest units of meaning in our language. Students can learn that words containing the same morphemes have similar meanings. For example, if students learn that the morpheme tele means distance and that the morpheme *phon* means sound, the students can infer that the word telephone means sound heard across a distance. When students learn that the morpheme *micro* means small and the morpheme *scope* means see, they will realize that a microscope enables an individual to see small objects. Building on their knowledge of morphemes, students will understand that a telescope helps an individual to see objects at a distance.

Students assimilate vocabulary more quickly when they can see the relationships between words. Ask the students to examine the words in their file boxes and on the word wall to find words that have the same morphemes. Then ask the students to use their understanding of the morphemes to infer the meanings of the new words. Make a chart in the classroom showing words with the same morphemes.

Organizing for Instruction *(cont.)*

Readers Theater

Consider using Readers Theater to give your students a memorable oral reading experience. Readers Theater provides an enjoyable opportunity for students to showcase their reading skills. The technique can be used with any work of realistic fiction.

Readers Theater is a technique that encourages students to read with expression. Students read selections aloud without using props or costumes. Emphasis is placed on the oral reading.

Before introducing this activity to the class, select portions of a realistic fiction selection that would be appropriate for dramatic oral reading. Scenes with a great deal of dialogue work well. You might choose a scene in which two characters argue or show strong emotion. A scene in which a character experiences a triumphant moment or suffers a loss might be a good choice for students to interpret.

After selecting the scenes, determine the number of students needed to read each scene. Divide the students into appropriate groups for Readers Theater.

Help each group choose a portion of the reading selection that they would like to dramatize.

Provide each student with a copy of the text to be used in the Readers Theater.

Highlight dialogue for each student. For example, In *Sarah, Plain and Tall,* Sarah's lines could be highlighted with a pink marker. Anna's lines could be highlighted with a blue marker. Caleb's lines could be highlighted with an orange marker.

The goal of Readers Theater is to present strong, dramatic reading. Encourage the students to use expression in their voices and fluent oral reading to interpret the story.

Name_____ date_____

References

McREL Standards

Copyright 2002 McREL, Mid-continent Research for Education and Learning. 2250 S. Parker Road, Suite 500, Aurora, CO 80014

Tompkins, Gail E. *Literacy for the 21st Century.* Merrill/Prentice Hall, 2002.

Children's Literature References

Anderson, Joan. *The First Thanksgiving Feast.* Clarion, 1984.

Avi. *Nothing But the Truth: A Documentary Novel.* Orchard, 1991.

——— *The Secret School.* Harcourt, Inc., 2001.

Ballard, Robert. *Exploring the Titanic.* Madison Publishing, 1988.

Bauer, Joan. *Rules of the Road.* Putnam's, 1998.

Bauer, Marion Dane. *A Question of Trust.* Scholastic, 1994.

Bawden, Nina. *The Robbers.* Lothrop, 1979.

Beirne, Barbara. *A Pianist's Debut: Preparing for the Concert Stage.* Carolrhoda, 1990.

Berger, Terry. *I Have Feelings.* Human Science, 1971.

Bial, Raymond. *Portrait of a Farm Family.* Houghton, 1995.

Blum, Mark. *Beneath the Sea in 3-D.* Chronicle, 1997.

Blumberg, Rhoda. *Shipwrecked: The True Adventures of a Japanese Boy.* Harper Collins, 2001.

Bourke, Linda and Sullivan, Mary Beth with Regan, Susan. *A Show of Hands: Say It In Sign Language.* Addison, 1980.

Bowen, Gary. *Stranded at Plimoth Plantation 1626.* Harper,1994.

Bunting, Eve. *Is Anybody There?* Harper, 1988.

Burns, Bree. *Harriet Tubman and the Fight Against Slavery.* Chelsea House Publishers, 1992.

Carbone, Elisa. *Stealing Freedom.* Alfred A. Knopf, 1998.

Carpenter, Frances. *The Elephant's Bathtub: Wonder Tales from the Far East.* Doubleday & Co., 1962.

Carter, Jimmy. *Always a Reckoning.* Random House, 1995.

Collier, J.L. & Collier, C. *With Every Drop of Blood.* Delacorte Press, 1992.

Christopher, Matt. *Catcher with a Glass Arm.* Little Brown & Co., 1991.

——— *The Lucky Baseball Bat.* Little Brown, & Co., 1991.

Conord, Bruce. *Cesar Chavez.* Chelsea, 1992.

Cushman, Karen. *The Ballad of Lucy Whipple.* Harper Collins, 1996.

Daigliesh, Alice. *The Courage of Sarah Noble.* Scribner's Sons, 1954.

Danziger, Paula. *The Cat Ate My Gymsuit.* The Putnam & Grosset Group, 1974.

Ellis, Neenah. *If I Live to Be 100: Lessons from the Centenarians.* Crown Publishing, 2002.

Farley, Walter. *The Black Stallion.* Random, 1941.

Fleischman, Sid. *By the Great Horn Spoon!* Little, Brown 1963.

Forbes, Esther. *Johnny Tremain.* Houghton Mifflin, 1943.

Freedman, Russell. *Lincoln: A Photobiography.* Clarion Books, 1987.

Fritz, Jean. *And Then What Happened, Paul Revere?.* Coward-McCann, 1973.

Gardiner, John Reynolds. *Stone Fox.* Thomas Y. Crowell, 1980.

Garland, Sherry. *Shadow of the Dragon.* Harcourt Brace, 1993 (1961).

George, Jean Craighead. *The Moon of the Bears.* HarperCollins, 1993.

The Talking Earth. Harper, 1983.

Giff, Patricia Reilly. *Pictures of Hollis Woods.* Random House, 2002.

Hunt, Irene. *Across Five Aprils.* Follet, 1964.

Iannone, Catherine. *Pocahontas.* Chelsea Juniors, 1996.

Jaffe, Steven H. *Who Were the Founding Fathers?: Two Hundred Years of Reinventing American History.* Holt, 1996.

Jurmain, Suzanne. *Once Upon a Horse: A History of Horses and How They Shaped Our History.* Lothrop, 1989.

Kalman, Bobbie. *A One-Room School.* Crabtree, 1994.

Kennedy, Caroline (editor). *Profiles in Courage for Our Time.* Hyperion, 2002.

Krementz, Jill. *How It Feels to be Adopted.* Knopf, 1982.

Lauber, Patricia. *The True or False Book of Cats.* National Geographic, 1998.

Lester, Helen. *Author: A True Story.* Houghton, 1997.

Lawlor, Laurie. *Addie's Long Summer.* Albert Whitman & Co., 1992.

——— *Gold in the Hills.* Walker and Co., 1995.

Lawrence, Iain. *The Wreckers*. Delacorte, 1998.

Levitin, Sonia. *Journey to America*. Simon & Schuster, 1970.

Lowry, Lois. *Number the Stars*. Houghton Mifflin, 1989.

Mills, Judie. *John F. Kennedy*. Watts, 1988.

McHugh, Elisabet. *Karen and Vicki*. Greenwillow, 1989.

———— *Karen's Sister*. Greenwillow, 1983.

MacLachlan, Patricia. *Caleb's Story*. Harper Collins, 2001.

———— *Sarah, Plain and Tall*. Harper Collins, 1985.

———— *Skylark*. Harper Collins, 1994.

Macy, Sue. *A Whole New Ball Game*. Penguin Books, 1993.

Montgomery, L.M. *Anne of Green Gables*. L.C. Page, 1908.

Myers, Walter Dean. *Hoops*. Bantam Doubleday Dell, 1983.

Naylor, Phyllis Reynolds. *Night Cry*. Atheneum, 1984.

O'Dell, Scott. *Island of the Blue Dolphins*. Dell, 1960. *Sarah Bishop*. Houghton Mifflin, 1980.

Olliver, Jane. *The Doubleday Christmas Treasury*. Doubleday & Co., 1986.

Paterson, Katherine. *Bridge to Terabithia*. HarperCollins, 1977.

———— *Jacob Have I Loved*. HarperCollins, 1980.

———— *Lyddie*. Dutton, 1991.

Ray, Delia. *Behind the Blue and Gray: The Soldier's Life in the Civil War*. Dutton, 1991.

Rawls, Wilson. *Where the Red Fern Grows*. Doubleday, 1961.

Ride, Sally and Okie, Susan. *To Space and Back*. Lothrop, 1986.

Rinaldi, Ann. *Amelia's War*. Scholastic, 1999.

Robinson, Barbara. *The Best Christmas Pageant Ever*. Avon, 1972

Rock, Gail. *The House Without a Christmas Tree*. Bantam, 1974.

———— *The Thanksgiving Treasure*. Bantam, 1974.

Rosenberg, Maxine B. *Growing Up Adopted*. Bradbury, 1989.

Sachar, Louis. *Holes*. Farrar, Straus & Giroux, 1998.

Schlein, Miriam. *Jane Goodall's Animal World: Elephants*. Atheneum, 1990.

Schroeder, Russell. *Disney's Mulan: Special Collector's Edition*. Disney Press, 1998.

Seuss, Theodore Geisel. *The Butter Battle Book*. Random House, 1984.

———— *The Cat in the Hat*. Random House, 1957.

———— *Did I Ever Tell You How Lucky You Are?* Random House, 1973.

———— *Green Eggs and Ham*. Random House, 1960.

———— *Horton Hatches the Egg*. Random House, 1940.

———— *How the Grinch Stole Christmas*. Random House, 1957.

———— *Hunches in Bunches*. Random House, 1982.

———— *I Had Trouble in Getting to Solla Sollew*. Random House, 1965.

———— *The Lorax*. Random House, 1971.

———— *McElligot's Pool*. Random House, 1947.

———— *Oh The Places You'll Go*. Random House, 1990.

———— *The Sneetches and Other Stories*. Random House, 1961.

———— *Thidwick, The Big Hearted Moose*. Random House, 1948.

———— *Yertle the Turtle and Other Stories*. Random House, 1958.

———— *You're Only Old Once*. Random House, 1986.

Shreve, Susan. *The Gift of the Girl Who Couldn't Hear*. Tambourine, 1991.

Silverstein, Alan and Virginia. *Dogs, All About Them*. Lothrop, Lee & Shepard Books, 1986.

Spinelli, Jerry. *Crash*. Random House, 1996.

———— *Loser*. Harper Collins, 2002.

———— *Maniac Magee*. Little Brown and Co., 1990.

Stevenson, Augusta. *Molly Pitcher, Young Patriot*. Aladdin Library, 1986.

Stock, Catherine. *Armien's Fishing Trip*. Morrow, 1990.

Taylor, Mildred. *Roll of Thunder, Hear My Cry*. Dial, 1976.

White, Sarah Gardiner. *Like Father, Like Son: Baseball's Major League Families*. Scholastic, 1993.

Williams, Barbara. *Titanic Crossing*. Dial Books, 1995.

Woodruff, Elvira. *The Christmas Doll*. Scholastic, 2000.

Wolf, Bernard. *Homeless*. Orchard, 1995.

Wolff, Virginia Euwer. *The Mozart Season*. Holt, 1991.

———— *Probably Still Nick Swansen*. Holt, 1988.

Yep, Laurence. *The Star Fisher*. Morrow, 1991.